FROM THE FILMS OF

Harry Potter

FROM THE FILMS OF

Harry Potter

FROM BUTTERBEER-INSPIRED CANDY
TO GOLDEN SNITCH CUPCAKES, 60 DELICIOUS RECIPES
INSPIRED BY THE HARRY POTTER FILMS

RECIPES BY VERONICA HINKE
WRITTEN BY KIM LAIDLAW

INSIGHT EDITIONS
SAN RAFAEL • LOS ANGELES • LONDON

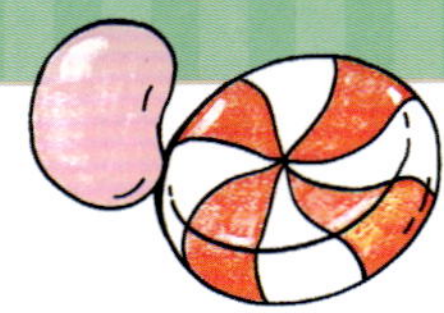

CONTENTS

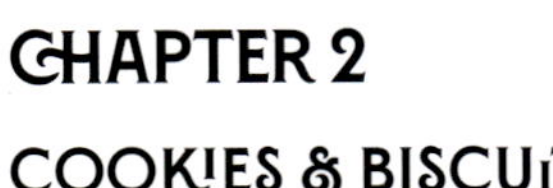

CHAPTER 4

PIES, TARTS & SWEET SAUCES

CHAPTER 5

DRINKS & FROZEN TREATS

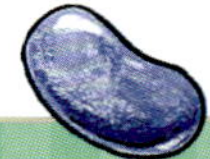

CHAPTER 6

BUTTERBEER-INSPIRED TREATS

FOR BUTTERBEER LOVERS

There are many recipes in this book that can be modified to include Butterbeer-inspired flavor with a few tweaks to your ingredients list (though, of course, nothing can quite compare to the real thing). Be on the lookout for these recommendations in the "For Butterbeer Lovers" sidebar of certain recipes. Cheers!

GRYFFIND

INTRODUCTION

Magic isn't just confined to wands, spells, or enchanted objects—it lives in the small, joyful moments, too, like unwrapping a sweet from Honeydukes, sneaking a treat from the Hogwarts feast, or sharing a homemade dessert with friends. This collection of recipes is crafted to capture that very essence, bringing the magic of the wizarding world's most beloved confections into your own kitchen.

As you flip through these pages, just imagine biting into a chewy Gummy Snake, its vibrant colors reminiscent of the shelves at Honeydukes, or savoring a piece of Gingery Treacle Tartlets, the golden, sticky dessert Harry Potter couldn't resist. Maybe you're more of a The Three Broomsticks White Chocolate Bark fan, with silky white chocolate swirled with crushed butterscotch candies, inviting you to join Harry, Hermione, and Ron at the Three Broomsticks for a quick sip. Or you can bake a batch of Gringotts Jewel Cookies, their bright red cherries gleaming like treasure. The treats in this book are sure to spark joy, like Chocolate Revivors, the rich chocolate bites designed to lift your spirits on the darkest days.

Remember, not all spells are cast with wands. Sometimes they're whisked into batter or stirred into a simmering pot. Take a sip of the Color-Changing Brew, an effervescent drink that shifts from deep blue to rich violet with a squeeze of fresh lemon, or pour a glass of chilled Honey-Roasted Pumpkin Patch Smoothie, as vibrant as Hagrid's pumpkin patch in autumn.

Of course, no magical gathering would be complete without cake. Hagrid knew that well when he presented Harry with his first-ever birthday cake, a lopsided, lovingly made creation scrawled with "Happee Birthdae Harry." Re-create that tender moment with Harry's Chocolate Birthdae Cake, complete with pink frosting and all its charming imperfections. It's not just a dessert; it's a symbol of friendship and belonging.

These recipes aren't just about re-creating food from the wizarding world—they're about capturing the heart of it. The feeling of home, the thrill of adventure, and the joy of sharing something magical with the people you love. So, tie on your apron, grab your whisk (or wand), and conjure a little fun, one recipe at a time.

CHAPTER 1
SWEETS

CANDY QUILLS

YIELD: 8 to 10 candy quills, depending on the size of the mold

Inspired by the sugar quills that are a favorite among Hogwarts students, these candy quills are bright, colorful, and perfect for any Harry Potter–themed party. But unlike the sugar quills found in the Harry Potter movies, you don't need to chase down the Honeydukes trolley or take a trip to Hogsmeade to enjoy these featherlight candies. Try adding your favorite flavorings to match the vibrant colors. Eat them on their own, use them to decorate a piece of cake or pie, or serve them as part of an assortment of other colorful, sugary treats.

- Cooking spray
- 1½ cups granulated sugar
- ¾ water
- ⅔ cup corn syrup
- ½ teaspoon cream of tartar
- 2 teaspoons liquid flavor extract or other liquid flavoring
- 4 to 6 drops liquid food coloring, less or more as desired

SPECIALTY TOOLS

- Candy thermometer
- Long feather (quill) silicone candy molds, measuring 3 to 4 inches long
- Glass tincture dropper

Spray the quill molds with cooking spray and set them on a baking sheet to keep them sturdy.

In a large saucepan over medium heat, combine the sugar, water, corn syrup, and cream of tartar. Bring the mixture to a boil; continue to cook until the temperature reaches 300°F on a candy thermometer.

Remove from heat and quickly stir in flavoring and food coloring of choice. Ensure the coloring is completely blended into the mixture and there are no streaks.

Use a glass tincture dropper to fill the cavities of the quill candy molds, or carefully pour the candy syrup into the molds. The candy syrup will be too hot for a plastic tincture dropper. Let the quill molds rest until the quills are completely hardened, about 45 minutes. When the quills are hardened, pull each quill out of its mold.

Separate each layer with plastic wrap or parchment paper until time to use.

"ANYTHING OFF THE TROLLEY, DEARS?"

—The Trolley Witch, *Harry Potter and the Sorcerer's Stone*

TOASTED COCONUT FROGS

YIELD: 6 to 8 frogs, depending on the size of the mold

These Toasted Coconut Frogs are an ode to the iconic Chocolate Frog wizarding treat that Ron and Harry love so much. You may remember Harry and Ron giddy with excitement when Harry opens his first Chocolate Frog on the Hogwarts Express in *Harry Potter and the Sorcerer's Stone*, unveiling the collectible card of Albus Dumbledore. These Chocolate Frogs, made with chewy toasted coconut in frog-shaped candy molds, won't hop out of the train window, but they'll certainly surprise and delight. Serve them on a plate of toasted coconut for an enchanting presentation.

- 3 tablespoons unsweetened coconut
- 3 cups semisweet chocolate wafers, divided
- 1 tablespoon coconut oil or olive oil
- Cooking spray

SPECIALTY TOOLS

- 1 sheet frog-shaped plastic candy molds

Preheat the oven to 350°F.

Spread the coconut in a thin layer inside a 9-inch-square baking dish. Bake the coconut in the oven until it becomes light brown, about 10 minutes. Watch the coconut closely to ensure it does not burn. Remove from the oven and set the toasted coconut aside to cool so it becomes crunchy.

In a double boiler over medium-low heat, or in a microwave-safe bowl in the microwave, melt 1 cup of chocolate wafers. If using a microwave, melt in 30-second bursts, stirring until smooth. Paint the inside of each frog cavity with the melted chocolate, completely coating it in a thin layer, creating a shell. Set aside to set, about 10 minutes.

In a double boiler over medium-low heat, or in a microwave-safe bowl in the microwave, combine the remaining 2 cups of chocolate and the oil and melt the chocolate. If using the microwave, microwave for 1 minute, stirring after 30 seconds. Add the toasted coconut and stir well to combine thoroughly.

Spray cooking spray inside the frog molds. Wipe away any excess with a soft cloth.

Using a spoon or small spatula, place the chocolate mixture into each of the frog molds. Spread the chocolate throughout each of the molds, ensuring that the chocolate is the same thickness all over.

Place the molds in the refrigerator until the chocolate is firm enough to be removed from the molds without breaking, about 4 hours.

Once set, carefully pull the chocolate from the molds. Arrange the frogs on a serving platter.

Store at room temperature in an airtight container for 5 to 6 days.

Albus Dumbledore
Albus Dumbledore
Frog

GREAT HALL LOLLIPOPS

YIELD: 12 lollipops

At the Hogwarts Halloween feast in *Harry Potter and the Sorcerer's Stone*, the Great Hall overflows with magical treats—roast meats, cakes, and towering sweets. Among the delights sit giant, swirled lollipops, their vibrant colors glistening under floating candles. But the festive atmosphere shatters when Professor Quirrell bursts in shouting, "Troll in the dungeon! Thought you ought to know . . ." before collapsing.

These smaller (albeit just as tasty) lollipops will transport you right back to the Great Hall with all your favorite Hogwarts friends, without the dungeon troll. Add your favorite flavors and enjoy!

- Cooking spray
- About 1 tablespoon each of sprinkles, colored sugar, or gold flakes of your choosing
- 1½ cups granulated sugar
- ¾ cup water
- ⅔ cup corn syrup
- ½ teaspoon cream of tartar
- ½ teaspoon liquid flavor extract or other liquid flavoring
- 6 to 8 drops liquid food coloring

SPECIALTY TOOLS

- Two (6-cavity) lollipop molds, suitable for hard candy (2-inch-diameter lollipops)
- Candy thermometer
- 12 (6-inch-long) lollipop sticks

"SILENCE. EVERYONE WILL PLEASE NOT PANIC. NOW PREFECTS WILL LEAD THEIR HOUSE BACK TO THE DORMITORIES. TEACHERS WILL FOLLOW ME TO THE DUNGEONS."

—Professor Albus Dumbledore, *Harry Potter and the Sorcerer's Stone*

Spray cooking spray inside the lollipop mold.

Sprinkle gold flakes, colored sugar, or sprinkles into each mold (or use them all!). In a large saucepan over medium heat, combine the sugar, water, corn syrup, cream of tartar, and liquid flavoring. Bring the mixture to a boil; continue to cook until the temperature reaches 300°F on a candy thermometer.

Remove from heat and quickly add the food coloring. Stir in the food coloring and pour the mixture into the molds. Place a lollipop stick into the bottom of each candy mold before it begins to harden. Sprinkle again with gold flakes and sprinkles so both sides of the lollipops are coated.

If presenting as a gift, wrap in clear plastic and tie a bow at the base of the candy where it meets the stick.

FOR BUTTERBEER LOVERS

Use butterscotch extract for flavoring and 8 to 10 drops of yellow food coloring.

FIZZY CHOCOLATE ROUNDS

YIELD: 6 to 8 rounds, depending on the size of the mold

Inspired by the enchanting Fizzing Whizzbees, these homemade chocolate rounds come with a delightful crunch. At Honeydukes, the famous Hogsmeade sweetshop where Fizzing Whizzbees were sold, these candies are known for their sherbet-like fizz and bubbling sensation, lifting the eater slightly off the ground. Though this version won't make you levitate, the crispy rice cereal and chocolate create a fun, effervescent treat.

- 1 teaspoon edible gold luster dust
- 3 cups semisweet chocolate wafers
- 1 tablespoon coconut oil or olive oil
- 3 tablespoons crispy rice cereal

SPECIALTY TOOLS

- 1 sheet 1-inch-round plastic candy molds

Dust the inside of each candy cavity with luster dust.

In a double boiler over medium-low heat, or in a microwave-safe bowl in the microwave, melt the chocolate and the oil. If using the microwave, microwave for 1 minute, stirring after 30 seconds.

Add the crispy rice cereal and stir well to combine thoroughly.

Spread the chocolate mixure throughout each of the molds, ensuring that the chocolate is the same thickness all over.

Place the molds in the refrigerator until the chocolate is firm enough to be removed from the molds without breaking, about 4 hours.

Once set, carefully pull the chocolate from the molds. Serve the rounds on a small plate with dessert or place a piece on top of each dessert plate.

FOR BUTTERBEER LOVERS

To make this Butterbeer, substitute butterscotch morsels in place of chocolate wafers.

"I LOVE MAGIC."

—Harry Potter, *Harry Potter and the Goblet of Fire*

GUMMY SNAKES

YIELD: 10 to 12 worms, depending on the size of the candy mold

Gummy Snakes are a delightful twist on classic gummy worms, like the ones displayed in *Harry Potter and the Prisoner of Azkaban* at Honeydukes sweetshop. In the film, the beloved Hogsmeade store is filled with enchanting sweets, including gummy snakes, making it a dream for any wizard with a sweet tooth. These Gummy Snakes capture the same chewy, fruity delight as their worm counterparts and can be enjoyed on their own or as a whimsical garnish. Whether draped over a dessert, curled around the rim of a cocktail glass, or simply eaten by the handful, they bring a playful charm to any occasion.

6 ounces flavored gelatin of your choice
Three ¼-ounce packets unflavored gelatin
⅔ cup water
Cooking spray

SPECIALTY TOOLS
2-inch-long silicone snake candy molds
Eye dropper or syringe

In a medium saucepan over medium heat, combine both gelatins with the water. Stir well to combine and to dissolve the powdered gelatin. Remove the gelatin from the heat and set aside until it is cool enough to work with, 5 to 10 minutes.

Spray the molds lightly with cooking spray, using a soft cloth to wipe away any excess spray.

When the mixture is cool enough to touch, using an eye dropper or syringe, fill each of the molds. Place the molds in the refrigerator until the snakes are solid, 20 to 30 minutes.

When the snakes are set, pull each one out of its mold. Place the snakes on top of plates of dessert or in arrangements of assorted sweets.

CHOCOLATE BUCKBEAK FEATHERS

YIELD: 50 small feathers, depending on the size of the feather mold

These Chocolate Buckbeak Feathers are a delicate, sweet treat that bring a touch of enchantment to any dessert table. Buckbeak, a majestic Hippogriff with the body of a horse and the wings and head of an eagle, is introduced in *Harry Potter and the Prisoner of Azkaban* and plays a vital role in helping Harry, Hermione, and Sirius escape the Dementors.

Later, when Harry receives his Firebolt broomstick from Sirius Black, a beautiful feather from Buckbeak accompanies it, and Hermione remarks, "This came with it," admiring its elegant appearance. Made by painting chocolate inside silicone candy molds shaped like feathers, these treats can be used as stunning garnishes for cakes or drinks, to enhance a larger dessert spread, or enjoyed on their own as a charming indulgence.

- One 12-ounce bag white chocolate chips
- 1 tablespoon olive oil or coconut oil
- Cooking spray
- About ½ teaspoon white luster dust (optional)

SPECIALTY TOOLS

- 1 sheet feather-shaped plastic candy molds
- Crafting or pastry brush

In a double boiler over medium-low heat, or in a microwave-safe bowl in the microwave, combine the chocolate and oil and melt the chocolate. If using the microwave, microwave for 1 minute, stirring after 30 seconds.

Spray cooking spray inside the chocolate molds. Wipe away any excess cooking spray with a soft cloth.

Using a spoon, place the chocolate into each of the feather molds. Spread the chocolate throughout each of the molds, ensuring that the chocolate is the same thickness all over. Press in around the edges so that all the chocolate is inside the mold.

Place the molds in the refrigerator until the chocolate is firm enough to be removed from the molds without breaking, about 4 hours.

Once set, carefully pull the chocolate from the molds. Using a crafting or pastry brush, gently brush the luster dust over the feathers. Arrange the chocolates on a serving platter.

FOR BUTTERBEER LOVERS

To turn these quills into Butterbeer-inspired feathers, use butterscotch morsels in place of chocolate chips.

"ISN'T HE BEAUTIFUL?
SAY HELLO TO BUCKBEAK."

—Rubeus Hagrid, *Harry Potter and the Prisoner of Azkaban*

GREAT PRUNE TRUFFLES

YIELD: 16 to 18 prune truffles

When Hagrid comes to take Harry to Hogwarts for the very first time in *Harry Potter and the Sorcerer's Stone*, he's met by the Dursleys in a most unwelcoming way. Inspired by Hagrid's iconic insult to Vernon Dursley—"Dry up, Dursley, yeh great prune!"—these rich, chocolaty treats might just turn even the sourest personalities sweet.

Soft, chewy prunes are enveloped in luscious chocolate, creating a decadent truffle with a deep, caramellike fruitiness. The velvety texture and delightful contrast between the natural sweetness of dried plums and the rich, slightly bitter snap of chocolate prove that even prunes can be quite tasty with the right spell—or recipe!

- 2 cups semisweet chocolate chips
- 1 tablespoon coconut oil or olive oil
- 16 to 18 whole prunes, pitted
- ½ cup walnuts, chopped (optional)

In a double boiler over medium-low heat, or in a microwave-safe bowl in the microwave, combine the chocolate and oil and melt the chocolate. If using the microwave, microwave for 1 minute, stirring after 30 seconds.

Dip each of the prunes into the melted chocolate, covering just the top one-quarter of the prune. Spread the nuts on parchment paper and dip each prune truffle into the nuts, partially or fully covering the chocolate coating the prune.

Place the prune truffles in the refrigerator until the chocolate is firm, 4 to 6 hours.

Once set, serve the prune truffles on a small plate with dessert or place one on top of each dessert plate.

"I DEMAND YOU LEAVE AT ONCE, SIR. YOU ARE BREAKING AND ENTERING!"

—Vernon Dursley, *Harry Potter and the Sorcerer's Stone*

AUNT MARGE BRANDY BALLS

YIELD: Fifty 1-inch balls

Vernon Dursley's sister, Aunt Marge, is infamous for her sharp tongue and her harsh treatment of Harry in *Harry Potter and the Prisoner of Azkaban*. During one memorable encounter, she taunts Harry about his parents and insults them once again over dinner. Her cruel words lead to Harry losing his cool and accidentally causing Aunt Marge to inflate like a balloon and float out the door, helplessly blustering.

Made with crushed digestive biscuits, chocolate chips, and a touch of brandy, these treats are rolled in slivered almonds for a delightful crunch.

- 4 cups crushed digestive biscuits
- 1 cup semisweet chocolate chips
- 1 tablespoon coconut oil or olive oil
- One 5-ounce can evaporated milk
- ¼ cup brandy or rum (optional)
- 3 cups crushed slivered almonds

In a food processor, pulse the digestive biscuits until they are crushed.

In a double boiler over medium-low heat, or in a microwave-safe bowl in the microwave, combine the chocolate and oil and melt the chocolate. If using the microwave, microwave for 1 minute, stirring after 30 seconds.

Stir the evaporated milk and crushed biscuits into the chocolate. If using the brandy, stir it in now. Use a spoon to stir to ensure all the crushed biscuits are coated with the chocolate mixture.

Form 1-inch balls with the mixture. Roll each ball in the almonds until thoroughly coated.

NOTE: While rolling, the brandy balls will be wet. After they are rolled in almonds, they will hold their shape. They will dry further after they are made.

HOGWARTS HOUSES TRUFFLES

YIELD: Twenty-four 1-inch truffles

These colorful truffles are a delicious tribute to the four Hogwarts houses. Made with a creamy blend of white chocolate chips and cream cheese, each truffle is flavored and colored to represent one of the iconic houses. Ravenclaw truffles are blue and bursting with chocolate flavor, whereas Slytherin truffles are green with a refreshing mint taste. Gryffindor truffles shine red with a bold cherry kick, and Hufflepuff truffles are yellow with zesty lemon. Once the truffles are shaped, they are rolled in sparkling sugar for an extra-magical touch. If you'd like, play around with different flavors of extract.

Ravenclaw: Blue (chocolate)
Slytherin: Green (mint)
Gryffindor: Red (cherry)
Hufflepuff: Yellow (lemon)

- 16 ounces white chocolate chips
- 4 ounces cream cheese, softened
- ¼ cup heavy (whipping) cream
- ¼ teaspoon chocolate extract
- ¼ teaspoon mint extract
- ¼ teaspoon cherry extract
- ¼ teaspoon lemon extract
- 2 drops blue liquid food coloring
- 2 drops green liquid food coloring
- 2 drops red liquid food coloring
- 2 drops yellow liquid food coloring
- 1 teaspoon blue sugar crystals or sprinkles
- 1 teaspoon green sugar crystals or sprinkles
- 1 teaspoon red sugar crystals or sprinkles
- 1 teaspoon yellow sugar crystals or sprinkles

In a double boiler over medium-low heat, or in a microwave-safe bowl in the microwave, melt the chocolate. If using the microwave, microwave for 1 minute, stirring after 30 seconds.

In the bowl of a stand mixer, or in a large bowl using a handheld mixer, blend together the cream cheese and heavy cream until well combined, 1 to 2 minutes.

With the mixer on medium speed, mix in the chocolate until well combined.

Divide the mixture into four equal sections. Add and stir the coloring and flavoring into each section of the mixture.

Cover each section with plastic and set in the refrigerator to firm, 2 to 3 hours.

Remove from the refrigerator and scoop 1-inch balls out of the truffle mixture. Roll each ball in the palm of your hands.

Place the sugars into four shallow bowls. Roll the mixture from each section in the sugar, ensuring that the same number of truffles in each section is coated well.

Store the truffles, keeping each color separate, in airtight containers in the refrigerator until it is time to serve. Serve them with an assortment of other treats or as an accent to a dessert.

"IT TAKES A GREAT DEAL OF BRAVERY TO STAND UP TO YOUR ENEMIES, BUT A GREAT DEAL MORE TO STAND UP TO YOUR FRIENDS."

—Professor Albus Dumbledore, *Harry Potter and the Sorcerer's Stone*

HOGWARTS
DRACO DORMIENS NUNQUAM TITILLANDUS
RAVENCL
RAVENCLAW
SLYTHERIN
HUFFLEPUFF
GRYFFINDOR

LIGHTNING BOLT CANDY MINTS

YIELD: 100 mints, depending on the size and shape of the mold

Harry Potter's lightning bolt scar is one of his most recognizable features, a lasting mark from the night Lord Voldemort's Killing Curse struck him as an infant. This scar became a symbol of his connection to Voldemort and his ultimate triumph over the Dark Lord. These Lightning Bolt Candy Mints pay tribute to that iconic mark with their bold shape. Made with powdered sugar, cream cheese, yellow food coloring, and mint flavoring, they can be shaped using small candy molds or cookie cutters. Soft, creamy, and cool, they make a perfect treat to enjoy on their own or as a decorative touch for cakes and desserts.

- 4 ounces cream cheese, softened
- 1 tablespoon butter, softened
- 4 cups powdered sugar, plus more as needed
- ¼ teaspoon peppermint extract
- ⅛ teaspoon vanilla extract
- 8 drops yellow food coloring

SPECIALTY TOOLS

1-inch lightning bolt–shaped cookie cutter or 1-inch candy mold

In the bowl of a stand mixer, or in a large bowl using a handheld mixer, beat the cream cheese and butter until well combined. Reduce the speed to low and slowly add the sugar. Beat until well combined.

Add the extracts and food coloring. Add more sugar if needed, until you have a doughlike texture.

Roll the mint dough into a ball and use a rolling pin to roll the dough into ¼-inch thickness. Use the cookie cutter or candy mold to cut out the lightning bolts.

Set the mints on parchment paper or waxed paper until they are dry enough to store, 4 to 6 hours.

Store the mints in an airtight container in the refrigerator for up to 1 week. Place parchment paper or waxed paper between each layer of mints.

Serve the mints on a small plate after a meal or add a pop of whimsy and flavor to the top of a dessert like the Knickerbocker Glory (page 126). These mints are fun to place on top of cream on a piece of pie or with an assortment of other candy treats.

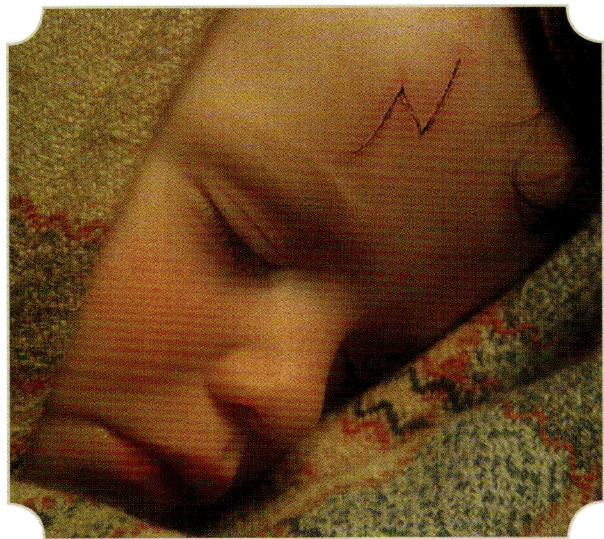

"THAT AIN'T NO ORDINARY CUT ON YOUR FOREHEAD, HARRY. A MARK LIKE THAT ONLY COMES FROM BEING TOUCHED BY A CURSE, AND AN EVIL CURSE AT THAT."

—Rubeus Hagrid, *Harry Potter and the Sorcerer's Stone*

SNOWBALL TRUFFLES

YIELD: Twenty-four 1-inch truffles

In *Harry Potter and the Prisoner of Azkaban*, when Draco Malfoy taunts Ron and Hermione near the Shrieking Shack, Harry, under the cover of his Invisibility Cloak, retaliates by throwing snowballs at Malfoy and his gang.

"Well, well, look who's here. You two shopping for your new dream home?" Malfoy sneers at Ron and Hermione before a snowball hits him in the face. Harry continues to tease them, sending the bullies running in fear. Unlike the bright, icy-cold snowballs from the scene, these white chocolate Snowball Truffles are sweet and soft. Coated in shredded sweetened coconut, they're a playful and satisfying bite to enjoy anytime, no Invisibility Cloak required.

- 16 ounces white chocolate chips
- 4 ounces cream cheese, softened
- ¼ cup heavy (whipping) cream
- ¼ teaspoon chocolate extract
- 2 cups sweetened coconut

In a double boiler over medium-low heat, or in a microwave-safe bowl in the microwave, melt the chocolate. If using the microwave, microwave for 1 minute, stirring after 30 seconds.

In the bowl of a stand mixer, or in a large bowl using a handheld mixer, blend together the cream cheese and heavy cream until well combined, 1 to 2 minutes. Add the melted chocolate and extract. Mix well on medium speed.

Cover your bowl with plastic and set in the refrigerator to firm, 2 to 3 hours.

Remove from the refrigerator and scoop 1-inch balls out of the truffle mixture. Roll each ball in the palm of your hands.

Place the coconut in a large, shallow bowl. Cover each ball by rolling it in the coconut.

Place the snowballs in the refrigerator until it is time to serve. Serve them with an assortment of other treats or as an accent to a dessert.

"BOYS, I THINK IT'S TIME WE TEACH WEASELBEE HOW TO RESPECT HIS SUPERIORS."

—Draco Malfoy, *Harry Potter and the Prisoner of Azkaban*

SORTING HAT FUDGE TREATS

YIELD: 24 bite-size pieces

These Sorting Hat Fudge Treats—complete with the iconic face—capture the magic of the Sorting Ceremony that happens for new students at Hogwarts. Though the hat quickly sorted Draco Malfoy into Slytherin and Ron and Hermione into Gryffindor, it paused over Harry, saying, "Hmmm, difficult. Very difficult. Plenty of courage, I see. Not a bad mind, either. There's talent, oh yes, and a thirst to prove yourself. But where to put you?" After Harry insisted, "Not Slytherin, not Slytherin," the Sorting Hat finally declared, "Well, if you're sure, better be . . . Gryffindor!"

These easy-to-make fudge treats use marshmallow crème and chocolate chips to keep their chewy and decadent form.

- 3 cups granulated sugar
- ¾ cups butter
- ⅔ cup evaporated milk
- 12 ounces chocolate chips
- 7 ounces marshmallow crème
- 1 cup mini marshmallows

SPECIALTY TOOLS

- 9-by-13-inch silicone jelly roll pan or similar-size baking pan
- Miniature wood dollhouse stools (sorting stools) (optional)

"WHEN I CALL YOUR NAME, YOU WILL COME FORTH. I SHALL PLACE THE SORTING HAT ON YOUR HEAD, AND YOU WILL BE SORTED INTO YOUR HOUSES."

—Professor Minerva McGonagall,
Harry Potter and the Sorcerer's Stone

Place a sheet of parchment paper in a 9-by-12-inch baking pan, ensuring that the paper goes up the sides of the pan.

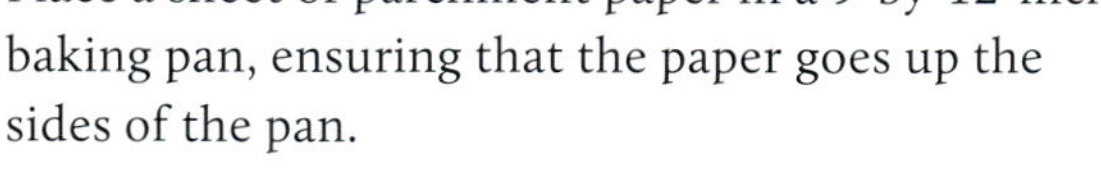

In a medium saucepan over high heat, combine the sugar, butter, and evaporated milk. Bring to a rolling boil. Continue to boil for 4 minutes, stirring the mixture constantly. Remove from heat and use a spoon to quickly mix in the chocolate. When the chocolate is thoroughly mixed in, add the marshmallow crème and combine well. Add the mini marshmallows and stir well until the marshmallows are melted and completely incorporated.

Pour about one-third of the fudge mixture into the jelly roll pan, spreading out with an offset spatula into even layer. Pour the remaining fudge mixture into the parchment-lined baking pan. Set both aside to cool and firm up, 2 to 3 hours.

Using about 1 tablespoon of fudge from the deeper pan, roll it into a cylinder, about ¾ inch by 1 inch. Continue to roll, putting pressure on one end to shape it into a point, and set the cone down on its flat end to level it. Once you have created all the cones, cut 1-inch-diameter circles from the thin layer of fudge. Use your fingers to gently thin out each circle, creating an organic hat brim, and press a cone onto each circle. Chill the hats for 20 to 30 minutes, then insert a knife angled down for both of the eyes. Then insert the knife below and create a wider slit for a mouth.

Place the fudge hats on three or four stools and arrange the other fudge hats around the stools. Store in an airtight container in the refrigerator or a cool place.

Candied Bacon Bites

YIELD: 25 to 30 bacon bites

Just like all the other meals at Hogwarts, the breakfast spread overflows with tasty treats that students just can't get enough of. From sweet to savory, there's a tasty morsel for every witch and wizard to start their day off right!

These Candied Bacon Bites would surely be a hit if served at Hogwarts. They consist of just two simple ingredients: thick slices of applewood-smoked bacon and brown sugar. The result is a perfect balance of sweet and salty, great for snacking on their own or as a topping for maple-iced cookies, cakes, or doughnuts.

½ pound (7 strips) applewood smoked bacon

¼ cup light brown sugar

Preheat the oven to 375°F.

Arrange the bacon on a 13-by-18-inch baking sheet lined with parchment paper. Sprinkle half the brown sugar on the bacon strips. Place the bacon in the oven and bake for 15 minutes.

Use tongs to turn each bacon strip over. Sprinkle the remainder of the brown sugar on the flip side of the bacon and cook for another 15 minutes.

Remove the bacon from the oven when it is browned well and pulling away from the sheet pan.

Set the bacon aside until it is cool enough to touch, 10 to 15 minutes. When cool enough to touch, slice the bacon into 1-inch pieces. Serve warm with other sweet treats or keep cool in the refrigerator for when ready to use.

SLUG CLUB CONFECTIONS

YIELD: Twenty-four 1-inch balls

Slug Club Confections are sweet, bite-size treats inspired by the "dragon balls" (aka dragon tartare) served by Professor Horace Slughorn at his Slug Club Christmas party in *Harry Potter and the Half-Blood Prince*. These round confections are made with a blend of dates, figs, and cocoa powder, creating a rich, chewy texture with just the right amount of sweetness.

Slughorn's appetizer was a hit at the party, though the dish was more about impressing guests than being appetizing (apparently, "they give one horribly bad breath"). Hermione attends the party with Cormac McLaggen, who is particularly obnoxious toward her, but Harry gets the best of Cormac by telling him the tartare is actually "dragon balls." These balls provide a less fiery but equally delightful treat, perfect for any occasion where flair and flavor are needed.

- 2 cups chopped dates
- 2 cups figs, trimmed and chopped
- ¼ cup instant hot cocoa powder

In a large mixing bowl, combine the dates and figs and roll the mixture into 1-inch balls.

Sprinkle the instant hot cocoa powder on parchment paper and roll each of the balls in the hot cocoa powder until thoroughly coated. This will remove much of the stickiness and add sweetness and flavor.

Serve the balls with an assortment of other sweet treats or accent a cake or piece of a special dessert.

"I DIDN'T GET INTO THE SLUG CLUB. IT'S OKAY, THOUGH. HE'S GOT BELBY HANDING OUT TOWELS IN THE LOO."

—Neville Longbottom, *Harry Potter and the Half-Blood Prince*

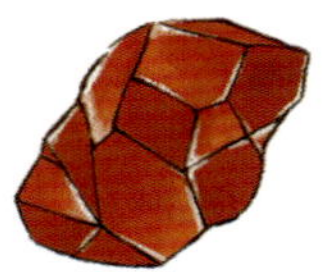

SORCERER'S STONE CANDIES

YIELD: Fifty 1-inch stones

These shiny red Sorcerer's Stone Candies are sure to capture the mystique of the legendary stone from *Harry Potter and the Sorcerer's Stone*. The real Sorcerer's Stone, a ruby-red alchemical marvel created by Nicolas Flamel, had the power to turn any metal into pure gold and produce the Elixir of Life, granting immortality. And Voldemort, using Professor Quirrell as a host, nearly succeeded in stealing it. Protected by enchantments and magical creatures—including Fluffy, the three-headed dog—the Stone was ultimately kept safe thanks to eleven-year-old Harry Potter. These candies are a sweet tribute to the magical object that started it all.

Cooking spray

1½ cups granulated sugar

¾ cup water

⅔ cup corn syrup

½ teaspoon cream of tartar

2 drops liquid flavor extract or other liquid flavoring

10 drops red food coloring

SPECIALTY TOOLS

Candy thermometer

Candy mold (shape of your choosing) (optional)

Kitchen mallet

Spray cooking spray in a square baking dish or candy mold.

In a large saucepan over medium heat, combine the sugar, water, corn syrup, and cream of tartar. Bring the mixture to a boil; continue to cook until the temperature reaches 300°F on a candy thermometer.

Remove from heat and quickly stir in the extract and food coloring. Ensure the coloring is completely blended into the mixture and there are no streaks.

Pour the mixture into the baking dish or mold. Set aside to allow the candy to harden, 10 to 15 minutes.

When the candy is hard, use a kitchen mallet on the baking dish candy to break it up into small pieces with defined edges like the edges of the Sorcerer's Stone.

Serve the candy stones as garnish on a dessert, with an assortment of candies, or in clear plastic bags for guests to take home with them.

"AIN'T NO ONE GONNA GET PAST FLUFFY. AIN'T A SOUL KNOWS HOW, 'CEPT FOR ME AND DUMBLEDORE."

—Rubeus Hagrid, *Harry Potter and the Sorcerer's Stone*

TREACLE LICORICE BITES

YIELD: 30 to 35 bite-size pieces

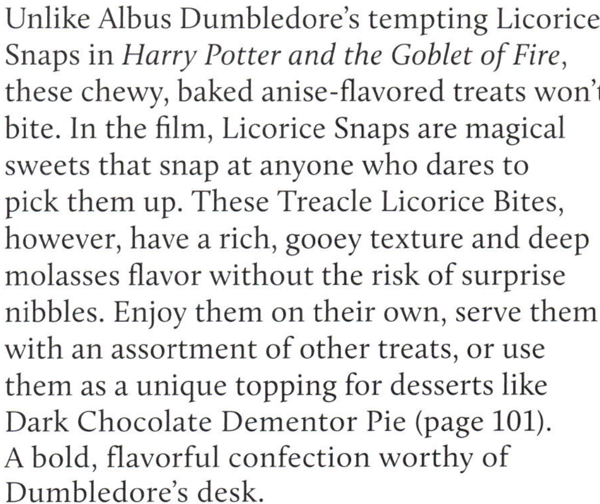

Unlike Albus Dumbledore's tempting Licorice Snaps in *Harry Potter and the Goblet of Fire*, these chewy, baked anise-flavored treats won't bite. In the film, Licorice Snaps are magical sweets that snap at anyone who dares to pick them up. These Treacle Licorice Bites, however, have a rich, gooey texture and deep molasses flavor without the risk of surprise nibbles. Enjoy them on their own, serve them with an assortment of other treats, or use them as a unique topping for desserts like Dark Chocolate Dementor Pie (page 101). A bold, flavorful confection worthy of Dumbledore's desk.

- ½ cup (1 stick) butter
- 1 cup granulated sugar
- ½ cup evaporated milk
- ½ cup dark corn syrup
- ¼ cup blackstrap molasses or treacle
- ¼ ounce (1 envelope) unflavored gelatin
- ¼ teaspoon coarse salt
- 1 cup all-purpose flour
- 2 teaspoons black gel food coloring
- 1 tablespoon anise extract

SPECIALTY TOOLS

Candy thermometer

In a large saucepan over medium heat, combine the butter, sugar, evaporated milk, corn syrup, molasses, gelatin, and salt. Stir constantly and bring to a low boil.

Remove from heat when the temperature of the mixture reads 240°F on a candy thermometer. Use a large spoon to quickly stir in the flour, food coloring, and anise extract.

Spread the mixture onto a 13-by-18-inch baking sheet lined with parchment paper. Let rest for 3 to 4 hours or overnight.

Use a paring knife to cut long strips of the licorice. Use your fingertips to gently but firmly twist each of the strips into a rope. Another option is to cut the licorice into 1-inch pieces that can be individually wrapped in small pieces of waxed paper.

Serve the licorice bites with an assortment of other flavorful treats or use them to decorate desserts like the Dark Chocolate Dementor Pie (page 101).

CHRISTMAS NUT BRITTLE

YIELD: 12 servings

Molly Weasley is known for her love of cooking and baking, often sending homemade treats and sweets to Harry and Ron. Molly's culinary care—and her love of gifting homespun sweaters—is always a reminder of her warm, nurturing spirit.

This nut brittle is inspired by Molly's culinary prowess and love for holiday spreads. Nut brittle is a British Christmas staple, and this one brings a little festiveness to any table with its combination of toasted almonds and pistachios.

- 1 cup granulated sugar
- ½ cup light corn syrup
- ¼ cup water
- ¼ teaspoon sea salt
- ¾ cup whole salted pistachios, shelled
- 1 teaspoon baking soda
- 1½ tablespoons butter, softened
- ¾ cup slivered almonds

SPECIALTY TOOLS

Candy thermometer

"OH, HARRY, HARRY! THERE YOU ARE. HAPPY CHRISTMAS. LOVELY TO HAVE YOU WITH US."

—Molly Weasley, *Harry Potter and the Order of the Phoenix*

In a medium saucepan over low-medium heat, combine the sugar, corn syrup, water, sea salt, and pistachios. Use a long-handled spoon to stir to combine the ingredients well, and continue stirring until the sugar dissolves.

Increase the heat to high and bring the mixture to a bubbling boil. Watch closely and stir occasionally to ensure the mixture does not burn.

Use a candy thermometer to watch the temperature. Continue to cook until the mixture reaches 320°F, about 15 minutes. Immediately remove the saucepan from the heat and set it on a cool burner on the stovetop. Quickly add the baking soda and butter, using the long-handled spoon to stir to combine. The mixture should be a golden-brown color. Add the almonds and stir to combine well.

Working quickly again, spread the mixture on a 13-by-18-inch baking sheet lined with parchment paper. Spread the mixture to about ⅛-inch thickness.

Let the mixture cool, about 1 to 3 hours or overnight.

When the brittle is cool and set, use your hands to break it up into 1-inch pieces. The pieces will have different shapes and sizes and jagged edges.

CHEWABLE CHOCOLATE CHEWS

YIELD: Thirty 1-inch pieces of taffy

Inspired by the delicious (albeit sticky) Unchewable Chew Chews created by Fred and George Weasley and sold in their Weasleys' Wizard Wheezes shop, these chocolate-flavored taffy chews are the perfect candy to give your jaw a workout. You can almost see these tasty treats neatly displayed in jars or wrapped in waxed paper on the shelves at their famous joke shop!

These chocolate candies are soft and chewy, with a subtly sweet and salty taste—that stretches endlessly and tangles playfully around your tongue. This chocolaty homemade treat is sure to spark some fun!

- 2 tablespoons plus 2 teaspoons butter, softened and divided
- 1 cup granulated sugar
- 1 tablespoon cornstarch
- ¾ cup light corn syrup
- 1 teaspoon pink Himalayan sea salt
- 1½ teaspoons chocolate flavoring
- ½ teaspoon vanilla extract
- ½ cup water

SPECIALTY TOOLS

Candy thermometer

"WE'D RECOMMEND THIS ONE. IT'S THE ONE-EYED WITCH PASSAGEWAY. IT'LL LEAD YOU STRAIGHT TO HONEYDUKES' CELLAR."

—Fred and George Weasley, showing Harry the Marauder's Map, *Harry Potter and the Prisoner of Azkaban*

With 1 teaspoon of butter, use your fingers to grease a 13-by-18-inch baking sheet lined with parchment paper.

In a saucepan over medium heat, combine the sugar, cornstarch, corn syrup, sea salt, 2 tablespoons of butter, the chocolate flavoring, vanilla, and water. Stir well to combine.

Place a candy thermometer on the side of the saucepan, attaching it with the clip. Bring the mixture to a boil. When the taffy reaches 250°F to 253°F, pull it from the stove.

Quickly and evenly spread the mixture throughout the baking sheet. Set aside until it is cool enough to touch and start pulling, 5 to 7 minutes.

With the remaining 1 teaspoon of butter, lightly and thoroughly grease your hands.

Form the taffy into a ball. Use both hands to pull the taffy out from the center on each side.

Constantly pull the taffy for 10 to 15 minutes. The taffy will start out looking silky and shiny, and as it is pulled, the texture will become smoother and the color will become lighter and duller.

Roll the taffy into a rope by rolling it between both hands. Use a paring knife to cut the taffy into 1-inch pieces.

Wrap each piece of taffy in 2-by-4-inch pieces of waxed paper. Allow enough room on the ends to twist the ends on both sides to create handles.

FOR BUTTERBEER LOVERS

To make Butterbeer-inspired chews, you can use ½ teaspoon of butterscotch extract and 1 teaspoon of vanilla extract instead of the chocolate flavoring.

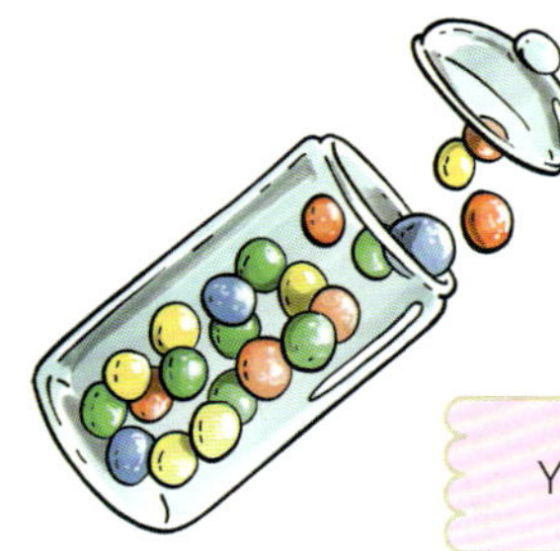

CHOCOLATE REVIVORS

YIELD: 12 to 16 molded chocolates, depending on the size of the mold

These chocolate treacle candies capture the restorative power of chocolate following Dementor encounters. Each bite of these treats melds rich chocolate with sweet treacle or molasses to soothe the soul and reinvigorate the senses.

"Here," Professor Lupin says to Harry in *Harry Potter and the Prisoner of Azkaban*, as he hands him an enormous slab of chocolate after a Dementor attack. "Eat this, it'll help."

"What . . . what was that thing that came?" Harry asks Lupin.

"It was a Dementor. One of the guards of Azkaban. Eat, you'll feel better," Lupin replies.

Harry takes a big bite of the chocolate, and to his great surprise, he feels better almost instantly. Throughout the movie, Professor Lupin relies on chocolate to help Harry recover from the Dementors' effects, mitigating the dread, despair, and physical cold while restoring warmth, energy, and normalcy with a sweet touch.

- 1 cup semisweet chocolate chips
- 1 tablespoon olive oil or coconut oil
- 1 tablespoon blackstrap molasses or treacle
- Cooking spray

SPECIALTY TOOLS

- 1-inch candy molds (or the shape of your choosing)

"YOU SORT OF WENT RIGID . . . WE THOUGHT MAYBE YOU WERE HAVING A FIT OR SOMETHING."

—Ron Weasley, *Harry Potter and the Prisoner of Azkaban*

In a double boiler over medium-low heat, or in a microwave-safe bowl in the microwave, combine the chocolate and oil and melt the chocolate. If using the microwave, microwave for 1 minute, stirring after 30 seconds. Add the blackstrap molasses and stir well to combine thoroughly.

Spray a very light coating of cooking spray inside the chocolate molds. Wipe away excess with a soft cloth.

Using a small spoon, place the chocolate mixture into each of the molds. Spread the chocolate throughout each of the molds, ensuring that the chocolate is the same thickness all over. Press in around the edges so that all the chocolate is inside the mold.

Place the molds in the refrigerator until the chocolate is firm enough to be removed from the molds without breaking, about 4 hours.

Once set, carefully pull the chocolates from the molds. Arrange the chocolates on a serving dish.

ENGLISH TOFFEE

YIELD: 12 to 15 servings

There's nothing quite like the taste of classic English toffee. It's an iconic flavor that even Dumbledore hopes for when choosing an Every-Flavour Bean to try—only to end up with a less-than-tasty earwax flavor.

This version of classic toffee is smooth, buttery, and encased in luscious chocolate and toasted almonds. The melt-in-your-mouth treat could be just as easily found on a tray at the Weasleys' Christmas gathering or during a Great Hall feast as it would be packaged in vibrant colors in a display at Honeydukes.

- 1 cup sugar
- ¼ teaspoon salt
- ¼ cup water
- ½ cup (1 stick) butter
- ¼ cup semisweet chocolate chips
- 7½ cups crushed almonds (about 4 ounces per piece), toasted (optional)

SPECIALTY TOOLS

Candy thermometer

In a medium saucepan over low-medium heat, combine the sugar, salt, water, and butter. Use a long-handled spoon to stir to combine well.

When the sugar is melted, increase the heat to medium-high. Watch closely, stirring occasionally, to ensure the mixture does not burn.

Cook until the mixture reaches 300°F, about 12 to 15 minutes. When the mixture reaches 300°F, immediately pull it from the heat, pour it onto a 13-by-18-inch baking sheet lined with parchment paper, and spread it evenly to ¼-inch thickness.

Sprinkle the chocolate chips on top of the hot toffee. When the chocolate has melted, use a spatula to quickly spread the chocolate in a thin layer on top of the toffee.

Sprinkle the almonds (if using) on top of the melted chocolate.

Let the toffee cool for at least 4 to 6 hours or overnight.

When the toffee is cool and set, use your hands to break it up into 1-inch pieces. The pieces will have different shapes and sizes and jagged edges.

"I COULD BE SAFE WITH A NICE TOFFEE. ALAS, EARWAX."

—Professor Albus Dumbledore,
Harry Potter and the Sorcerer's Stone

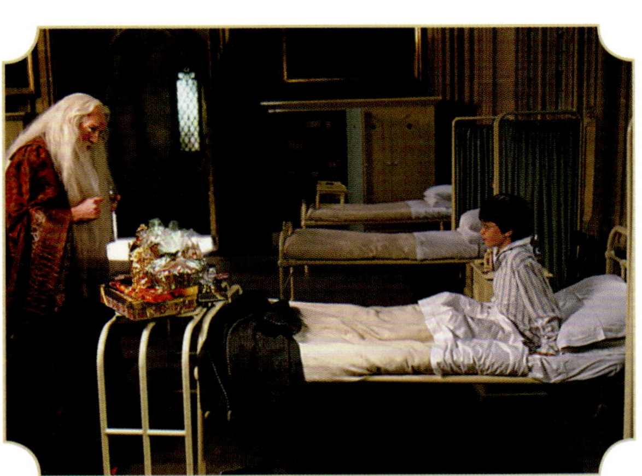

CHAPTER 2

COOKIES & BISCUITS

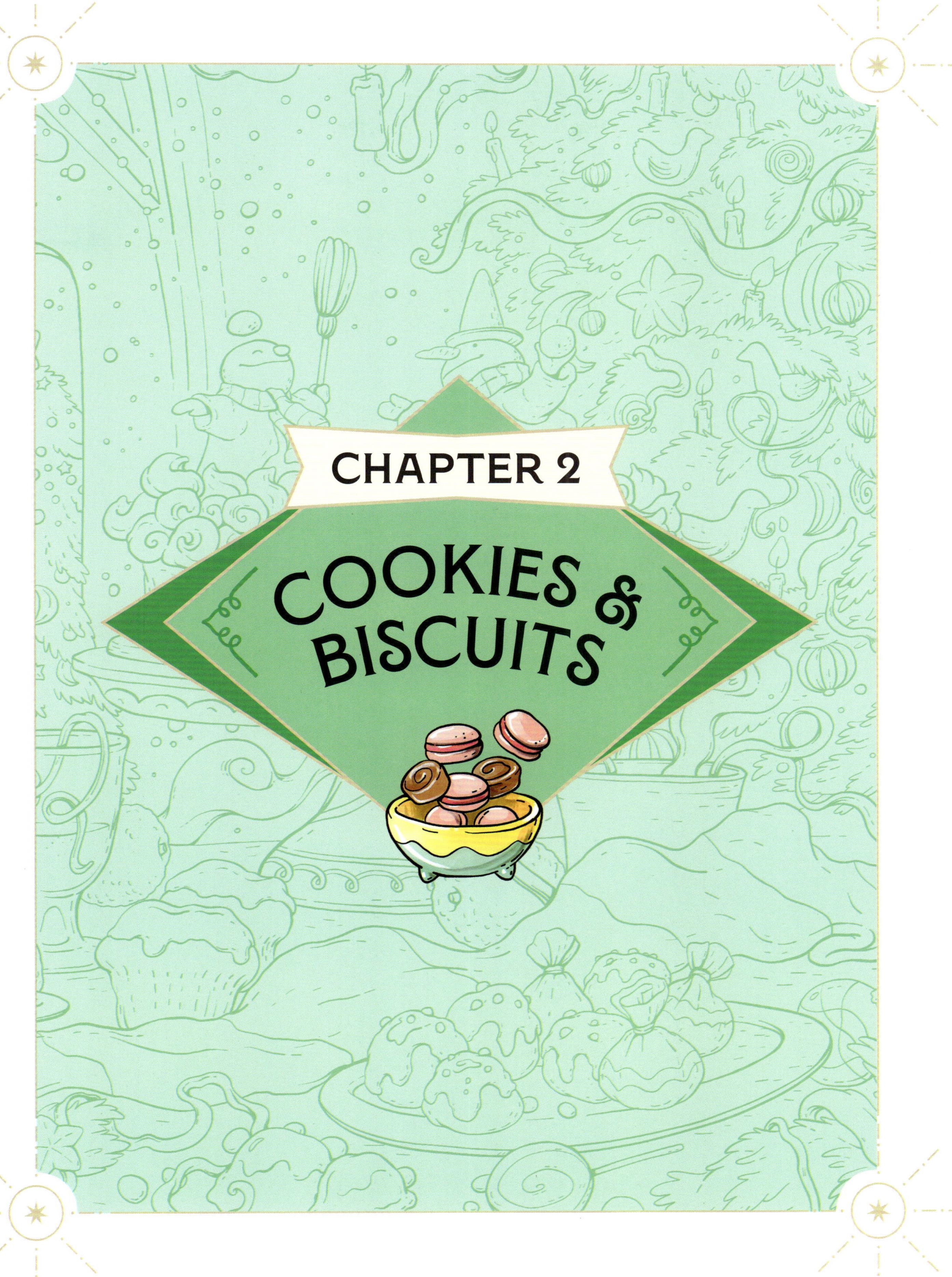

DEATHLY HALLOWS COOKIES

YIELD: 12 cookies

These classic English jam-filled sandwich cookies pay sweet homage to the legend of the Deathly Hallows. The top cookie is cut to resemble the Deathly Hallows—a triangle enclosing a circle and vertical line—representing the Elder Wand, Resurrection Stone, and Cloak of Invisibility. Sandwiching raspberry jam and topped with a chocolate wand, these treats are both symbolic and delicious.

According to wizarding lore, the Deathly Hallows were three powerful magical objects created by Death and gifted to the Peverell brothers, and uniting these objects was said to make one the Master of Death. Whether you're drawn to the legend or simply love a good biscuit, these treats bring a bit of sweetness to teatime.

2 cups all-purpose flour, plus more for dusting

½ cup granulated sugar

¼ teaspoon pink Himalayan sea salt

1 cup (2 sticks) butter, cold, cut into tiny pieces

1 large egg yolk

1 tablespoon water

1 vanilla bean pod

1 cup semisweet chocolate chips

1 cup raspberry jam

About ½ cup powdered sugar

SPECIALTY ITEMS

Triangle cookie cutter, 3½ by 3½ by 3½ inches

One 1¼-inch-diameter circle cookie cutter

"TOGETHER, THEY MAKE THE DEATHLY HALLOWS. TOGETHER, THEY MAKE ONE MASTER OF DEATH."

—Xenophilius Lovegood,
Harry Potter and the Deathly Hallows (Part 1)

In a large mixing bowl, combine 2 cups of flour, the granulated sugar, and sea salt.

Add the butter. Using your hands, mix the ingredients together until the dough forms and becomes coarse and crumbly.

Add the egg yolk and water.

Use a paring knife to open the vanilla bean pod and scrape the vanilla from the pod. Discard the pod or save to use with another recipe. Add the vanilla to the other ingredients.

Use your hands to mix the dough well. Form the dough into a ball and cover it with plastic wrap. Place the dough in the refrigerator until it firms up a bit, about 15 to 20 minutes. While the dough is chilling, preheat the oven to 375°F.

Dust a cutting board or silicone mat with flour and use a rolling pin to roll out the dough ⅛ inch thick.

Use the cookie cutter to cut out 24 triangle shapes. Cut a circle into the center of 12 of the triangle shapes.

Place the cookies on a 13-by-18-inch baking sheet lined with parchment paper. Bake for 10 to 12 minutes or until the edges are just beginning to brown.

While the cookies are baking, make the chocolate wands. In a double boiler over medium-low heat, or in a microwave-safe bowl in the microwave, melt the chocolate. If using the microwave, microwave for 1 minute, stirring after 30 seconds. Line a baking sheet with parchment paper and set aside.

Stir well with a spoon, making sure there are no lumps in the chocolate. Place the melted chocolate into a pastry bag and cut a small hole in the tip. Pipe 3-inch-long thin lines of chocolate on the parchment paper. Set the chocolate aside to harden, 20 to 30 minutes.

Remove the cookies from the oven and set them on a cooling rack to cool. After they have cooled for 15 to 20 minutes, use an offset spatula or table knife to spread a thin layer of the jam on the triangle cookies without the open circle. Place a triangle cookie with an open circle (a "window cookie") on top of each of the other triangles.

Use a fine-mesh strainer to sprinkle with powdered sugar.

When the chocolate wands have hardened, carefully lift them up from the parchment paper and place a chocolate wand vertically across the center of the cookie.

GALLEON COOKIES

YIELD: 24 cookies

In *Harry Potter and the Sorcerer's Stone*, Hagrid shows Harry the treasure trove of gold and silver coins his parents left for him at Gringotts Wizarding Bank, and Harry's eyes grow wide. "Din' think yer dad and mum would leave yeh with nothin' now, did yeh?" says Hagrid. Later, on the Hogwarts Express, Harry and Ron are offered treats by the Trolley Witch, and it's Ron's turn to get wide-eyed when Harry responds, "We'll take the lot."

These lemon-flavored Galleon Cookies celebrate that magical moment when Ron and Harry fill their stomachs with all the sweet treats they could want. With edible gold luster dust and nonpareils, these cookies are shaped like the wizarding world's glittering currency, making them the perfect sweet treat when you're feeling rich.

- 2 cups all-purpose flour
- 1¼ teaspoons baking soda
- ¼ teaspoon salt
- 1 cup granulated sugar
- ½ cup butter
- 1½ teaspoons vanilla extract
- 1 large egg, room temperature
- Juice and zest of 1 lemon, divided
- 1 teaspoon yellow food coloring
- ¾ cup whole milk
- 1 teaspoon edible gold luster dust and nonpareils

Preheat the oven to 350°F.

Line a 13-by-18-inch baking sheet with parchment paper.

In a large bowl, combine the flour, baking soda, and salt until well blended. Set aside.

In the bowl of a stand mixer or a large bowl with a hand mixer on high speed, cream together the sugar and butter until light, fluffy, and well blended. Mix in the vanilla, egg, lemon juice, lemon zest, and the food coloring; combine well.

Beat in half of the flour mixture, followed by half of the milk, and then repeat until everything is incorporated and blended well.

Use a small ice-cream scoop to create balls with the dough. Place the balls of dough 2 inches apart on the prepared baking sheet. Bake until firm and a little bit browned around the edges, 10 to 15 minutes. Remove from the oven and set aside to cool. Sprinkle with gold luster dust and nonpareils before serving.

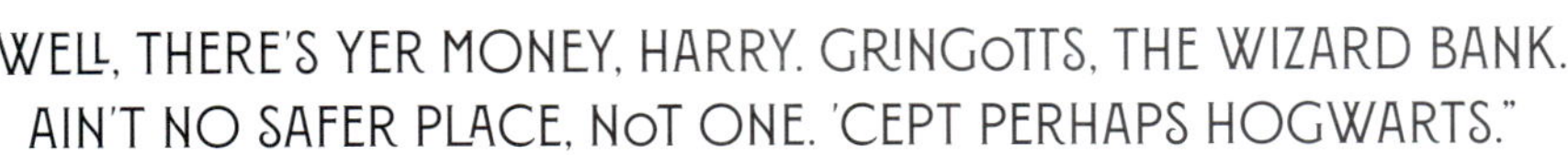

"WELL, THERE'S YER MONEY, HARRY. GRINGOTTS, THE WIZARD BANK. AIN'T NO SAFER PLACE, NOT ONE. 'CEPT PERHAPS HOGWARTS."

—Rubeus Hagrid, *Harry Potter and the Sorcerer's Stone*

PIXIE WING COOKIES

YIELD: 36 cookies

Cornish Pixies are mischievous blue little creatures that love wreaking havoc on their surroundings. Harry, Ron, Hermione, and Neville learned this the hard way in *Harry Potter and the Chamber of Secrets* when Professor Lockhart released pixies in his classroom as part of a Defense Against the Dark Arts lesson. The classroom descended into total chaos before the pixies were finally subdued.

Inspired by these troublesome creatures, these Pixie Wing Cookies are crisp, golden, and lightly dusted with powdered sugar. The deep-fried pastries are folded and twisted into delicate shapes before frying and are as cute as they are tasty!

- 3 small eggs or 2 large eggs
- ½ cup granulated sugar
- 1 tablespoon brandy or cognac (optional)
- 3 tablespoons butter, melted
- ⅓ cup Whipped Cream (page 148)
- 2 cups all-purpose flour
- ½ teaspoon baking powder
- ½ teaspoon ground cardamom
- ¼ teaspoon grated nutmeg
- ½ teaspoon pink Himalayan sea salt
- 10 cups (two 40-ounce bottles) vegetable oil, for frying the cookies
- 3 cups powdered sugar

SPECIALTY TOOLS

- Fattigmann cutter or pizza or pastry cutter
- Nutmeg grater (optional)

In the bowl of a stand mixer, or in a large bowl with a handheld mixer, beat the eggs, granulated sugar, and brandy (if using) on high speed until creamed, 1 to 2 minutes.

Add the melted butter and use a spoon to mix the butter with the creamed mixture. Carefully fold in the whipped cream.

Add the flour, baking powder, cardamom, nutmeg, and sea salt. Use your hands to mix the dough, combining everything well.

Form a large ball with the dough and cover it with plastic wrap. Place the dough in the refrigerator for at least 30 to 60 minutes or overnight.

Use a rolling pin to roll out the dough to about ¼ inch thick.

Use the cutter to cut the dough into diamond shapes, about 1¼ inches wide and 3½ inches long.

With a paring knife, cut a ½-inch-long slit in the middle of each diamond.

Bring the top corner of each of the diamonds down and pull it through the slit in the middle. Bring the other corner up. Now the cookie will be in the shape of a knot. Place the cookies on baking sheets and set them in the refrigerator to keep cool until the oil is hot enough to fry them.

"FRESHLY CAUGHT CORNISH PIXIES. LAUGH IF YOU WILL, MR. FINNIGAN, BUT PIXIES CAN BE DEVILISHLY TRICKY LITTLE BLIGHTERS. LET'S SEE WHAT YOU MAKE OF THEM, NOW! COME ON NOW, ROUND THEM UP, ROUND THEM UP! THEY'RE ONLY PIXIES!"

—Professor Gilderoy Lockhart, *Harry Potter and the Chamber of Secrets*

Pour the oil into a Dutch oven or another pan with a heavy bottom. Over medium heat, heat the oil to 375°F.

Fry the cookies in batches of six to eight at a time. Use a metal slotted spoon to gently turn the cookies a few times while they are frying. Fry the cookies until they are golden brown, 12 to 15 minutes. It is possible to burn the cookies, so watch them carefully and keep the heat at 375°F.

Pull the cookies from the oil and place them on a plate lined with paper towels.

When the cookies are cool enough to touch, spread the powdered sugar on a plate and delicately coat the cookies in the powdered sugar.

NOTE: That not all 3 cups of powdered sugar will be used on the cookies, but that much is necessary for coating the cookies in the sugar.

SAFE FRYING PRACTICES

- Whatever you use for frying (a fryer or Dutch oven), make sure it has a lid that fits well so it can be quickly covered in case of fire. Keep the lid handy.
- Never leave hot oil unattended while in use.
- Never move a fryer with hot oil in it.
- Do not fill the fryer more than one-third with oil.
- Carefully place foods into the hot oil in a way so that it does not splatter.
- Wear protective glasses.
- Overcrowding the fryer can cause food to be undercooked, which can cause food safety concerns.
- Cooking oil is highly flammable. Be very careful not to let oil come in contact with flames.
- Never use water to put out a grease fire. Use a fire extinguisher or cover with a lid.
- Dry foods completely before placing them in the fryer.
- Have a long-handled spider, high-heat spatula, or high-heat slotted spoon ready to use to turn foods and remove them from the fryer.
- Prepare plates lined with paper towels and have them ready to place foods as they are pulled from the fryer.
- Ensure oil has completely cooled before disposing of it.

ACROMANTULA COOKIES

YIELD: 36 cookies

These chocolate shortbread cookies with pretzel legs pay homage to Aragog, the giant Acromantula who ruled over a colony of spiders in the Forbidden Forest. In *Harry Potter and the Chamber of Secrets*, Harry and Ron seek out Aragog to clear Hagrid's name, only to find themselves trapped as Aragog's children close in, eager for fresh meat. Just as all hope seems lost, the enchanted flying car roars in to rescue them. With their spindly legs and deep chocolate flavor, these cookies bring to life one of the most suspenseful moments in the series.

- 1 cup powdered sugar
- 1 cup (2 sticks) butter, softened
- 2 cups all-purpose flour
- ½ cup cocoa powder
- ¼ teaspoon pink Himalayan sea salt
- 50 small, round, salted pretzels

Preheat the oven to 325°F.

In the bowl of a stand mixer, or in a large bowl with a handheld mixer, cream the sugar and butter, mixing on high speed for 1 to 2 minutes.

Add the flour, cocoa powder, and sea salt and beat on low speed. When the dry ingredients are blended, increase the speed to medium-high.

When the dry ingredients are completely blended in, wrap the dough in plastic wrap and place in the refrigerator for at least 1 to 2 hours or overnight.

Line a 13-by-18-inch baking sheet with parchment paper.

Use your hands to roll 1½-inch balls of the dough. Place the balls 1½ inches apart on the baking sheet. Use a sharp paring knife to snap apart the pieces of the pretzels for the legs. Gently press eight pretzel pieces into each ball, four on each side, creating Aragog's legs.

Bake the cookies until the cookies are firm on top, about 20 minutes.

Remove the cookies from the oven and set aside to cool. Once cool, carefully store in an airtight container, in a single layer, until ready to serve.

Serve the cookies on a tray with an assortment of other treats, or use them to decorate cakes or garnish slices of pies or cakes or scoops of ice cream.

"GO? I THINK NOT. MY SONS AND DAUGHTERS DO NOT HARM HAGRID ON MY COMMAND. BUT I CANNOT DENY THEM FRESH MEAT WHEN IT WANDERS SO WILLINGLY INTO OUR MIDST. GOODBYE, FRIEND OF HAGRID."

—Aragog, *Harry Potter and the Chamber of Secrets*

GRINGOTTS JEWEL COOKIES

YIELD: 24 cookies

These bright red, cherry-studded vanilla shortbread cookies, rolled into logs and sliced into ¼-inch rounds, find their inspiration in the shiny red gems guarded by goblins in Gringotts. Renowned for its advanced security measures, Gringotts is the only bank in the wizarding world and is home to highly protected vaults full of Galleons as well as rubies, emeralds, sapphires, yellow gems, and diamonds. Though Harry visits Gringotts a few times in the movies, his most explosive drop-in happens in *Harry Potter and the Deathly Hallows (Part 2)*, when Harry, Ron, and Hermione escape Gringotts on the back of its security dragon. Talk about making an exit!

These cherry-filled cookies are as visually striking as they are tasty and are the perfect way to celebrate any occasion.

- 1 cup brown sugar
- 1 cup granulated sugar
- 1½ cups shortening
- ¼ teaspoon pink Himalayan sea salt
- 1 teaspoon vanilla extract
- 1 teaspoon baking soda
- 1 teaspoon baking powder
- 3½ cups all-purpose flour
- 1 cup candied or maraschino cherries

At least 2 hours before baking, in a large bowl, combine the brown sugar, granulated sugar, shortening, sea salt, vanilla, baking soda, baking powder, flour, and cherries. Use your hand to mix well.

Form the cookie dough into two long cylindrical shapes. Place each on a piece of plastic wrap and roll the plastic wrap around the dough.

Put the cookie dough in the refrigerator for at least 2 hours or overnight.

When it is time to bake the cookies, preheat the oven to 375°F.

Remove the cookie dough from the refrigerator and use a small knife to slice the dough into ½-inch cookies.

Place the cookies on a 13-by-18-inch baking sheet lined with parchment paper. Ensure there is 1 inch between each cookie.

Bake the cookies until they are golden brown, about 15 minutes.

NOTE: If using maraschino cherries, drain them and lay them out on a paper towel–lined plate to dry before adding to the dough.

"CLEVER AS THEY COME, GOBLINS, BUT NOT THE MOST FRIENDLY BEASTS. BETTER STAY CLOSE."

—Rubeus Hagrid, *Harry Potter and the Sorcerer's Stone*

DOUBLE-GINGER NEWT BISCUITS

YIELD: 12 cookies

These delicious ginger biscuits draw inspiration from an English treat known as Ginger Nuts, a classic ginger snap cookie. This version comes in the shape of a newt, the slippery amphibian used in a variety of transfiguration spells that Hogwarts students learn about in Professor McGonagall's class. These Double-Ginger Newt Biscuits have a bold combination of ground ginger, chopped crystallized ginger, and a touch of molasses for depth. The result is a warmly spiced, slightly chewy biscuit with a crisp edge, perfect for enjoying with tea.

- 2½ cups all-purpose flour, plus more for dusting
- 1½ teaspoons baking soda
- ½ teaspoon baking powder
- ¼ teaspoon pink Himalayan sea salt
- ¼ teaspoon ground cinnamon
- 1½ tablespoons ground ginger
- ¼ teaspoon ground cardamom
- Pinch ground cloves
- ½ cup crystallized ginger, finely chopped
- ½ cup butter, softened
- ½ cup vegetable shortening
- 1 cup granulated sugar
- ¼ cup brown sugar
- 1 large egg
- 3 tablespoons molasses
- 1 vanilla bean pod

SPECIALTY TOOLS

Newt (lizard; gecko) cookie cutter, about 4 inches by 2¼ inches

Preheat the oven to 350°F.

In a large bowl, combine the flour, baking soda, baking powder, sea salt, cinnamon, ground ginger, cardamom, and cloves. Add the crystallized ginger and stir to combine well.

In the bowl of a stand mixer, or in a large bowl with a handheld mixer, cream the butter, shortening, and sugars until light and fluffy, 2 to 3 minutes. Add the egg and molasses.

Use a paring knife to open the vanilla bean pod and scrape the vanilla from the pod. Discard the pod or save to use in another recipe. Add the vanilla from the pod to the wet ingredients and stir well to combine.

Slowly add the dry ingredients to the wet and mix well to combine all the ingredients thoroughly. Form the dough into a ball and cover with plastic wrap or parchment paper. Set in the refrigerator for 30 minutes or overnight.

Remove the dough from the refrigerator.

Sprinkle flour on a cutting board or silicone baking mat and use a rolling pin to roll out the dough ¼ inch thick.

Use the cookie cutter to cut out newt shapes in the cookie dough. Gather up the remnants that remain after the cookies have been cut and roll those into a ball of dough for the next batch of cookies.

Place the cookies on a 13-by-18-inch baking sheet lined with parchment paper.

Bake the cookies in the oven until they are just slightly browned, 10 to 12 minutes.

Remove the cookies from the oven and set them aside to cool. Store in a sealed container for up to 1 week.

OCEANIC

MR H POTTER
The Cupboard
Privet Drive
Little Whinging
SURREY
HA

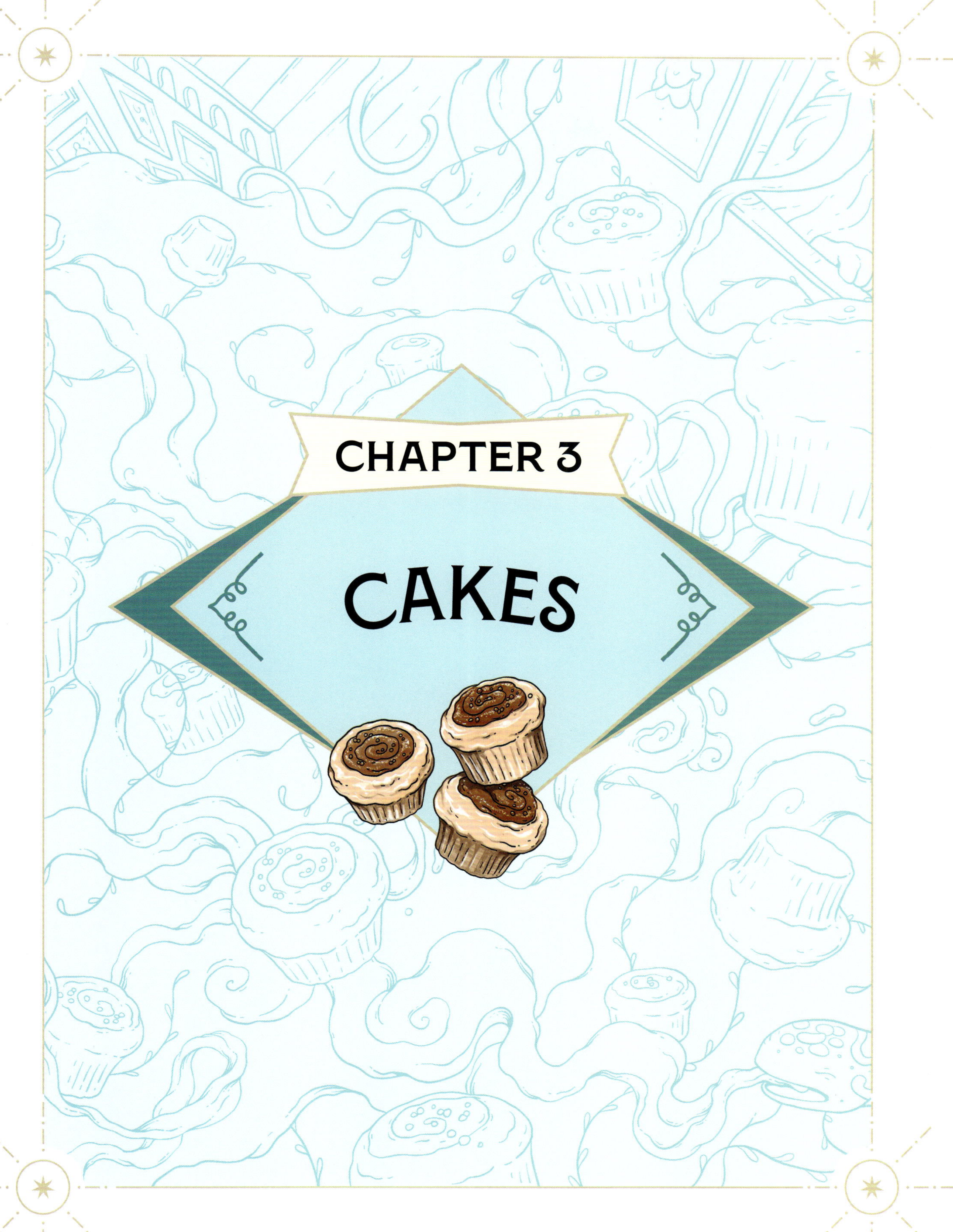
CHAPTER 3
CAKES

PARSELTONGUE SNAKE CAKE

YIELD: 16 servings

This cake is inspired by the unforgettable scene in *Harry Potter and the Sorcerer's Stone* when Harry strikes up a conversation with a Burmese python at the zoo on Dudley's eleventh birthday. As Harry says to the snake, "You're from Burma, aren't you? Was it nice there? Do you miss your family?" the two connect over their shared sense of being kept in captivity. When Dudley interferes in the conversation, Harry's anger triggers a magical response that makes the glass separating the snake from the observers vanish, sending Dudley tumbling into the tank. The snake then floats free, thanking Harry with a simple "Thanksssss."

This 3D cake is made from two vanilla–cream cheese Bundt cakes, with the head, neck, and tail crafted from crispy rice cereal and marshmallows. Fondant and metallic cake sprays bring the python to life. It's the perfect addition to your Harry Potter–themed party!

"I'M WARNING YOU NOW, BOY. ANY FUNNY BUSINESS, ANY AT ALL, AND YOU WON'T HAVE ANY MEALS FOR A WEEK."

—Vernon Dursley, *Harry Potter and the Sorcerer's Stone*

CAKE (THIS IS A DOUBLE BATCH TO MAKE 2 BUNDT CAKES):

- 3 cups plus 4 tablespoons butter, softened and divided
- 16 ounces cream cheese, softened and divided
- 6 cups granulated sugar, divided
- 2 vanilla bean pods, divided
- 12 large eggs, room temperature, divided
- 6 cups all-purpose flour, divided
- 2 teaspoons baking powder, divided
- ½ teaspoon sea salt, divided

CRISPY RICE CEREAL AND MARSHMALLOW TREATS:

- ½ cup (1 stick) butter, softened and divided
- 4 cups marshmallows
- 5 cups crispy rice cereal

FOR DECORATION:

- 18 ounces beige- or warm sand-colored cake icing fondant
- 1 recipe Buttercream Frosting (page 149)
- 1 tablespoon black cake icing fondant
- 1 tablespoon yellow cake icing fondant
- 1 teaspoon red cake icing fondant
- Gold cake-decorating luster spray
- 1 tablespoon bronze-colored cake-decorating luster dust
- 2 tablespoons black cookie icing (use the icing that is of the consistency for flooding cookies when decorating)

SPECIALTY TOOLS

- 12-cup fluted or straight-sided Bundt cake pan
- 4-by-5-inch snakeskin silk-screen stencil or webbed plastic onion or citrus bag

Preheat the oven to 350°F.

Grease the inside of the Bundt cake pan with 2 tablespoons of butter.

In the bowl of a stand mixer, or in a large bowl with a handheld mixer, cream 1½ cups of butter and 8 ounces of cream cheese on high speed for 1 to 2 minutes. Continue beating while slowly adding 3 cups of sugar. Beat on high speed 1 to 2 minutes.

Using a paring knife, open a vanilla bean pod and scrape the inside. Add the vanilla and beat for another minute.

Reduce the speed to low and add 6 eggs, one at a time. Add 3 cups of flour, 1 teaspoon of baking powder, and ¼ teaspoon of sea salt and mix at medium speed just until well combined.

Pour the cake batter into the loaf pan and bake in the oven until a toothpick comes out of the center clean, 75 to 90 minutes.

Remove the cake and set aside to cool, about 1 hour.

NOTE: Repeat these steps using the remaining ingredients to make two Bundt cakes.
OPTION: Make one small python cake with just one Bundt cake and a smaller python head and tail.

TO MAKE THE CRISPY RICE HYPHENATE: CEREAL-AND-MARSHMALLOW PYTHON HEAD, NECK, AND TAIL:

In a large saucepan over low heat, melt ¼ cup of butter. Add the marshmallows and stir until they are melted. Remove the marshmallow mixture from the heat and add the cereal. Stir to combine well.

When the mixture has cooled enough to touch, use the remaining ¼ cup of butter to butter your hands to form the python head and tail. For the neck, form a 12-inch-long rope that is wider and broader at the top for the head. For the tail, form a 12-inch-long rope that narrows into a tip at the end.

TO DECORATE:

Use a rolling pin to roll out the fondant on parchment paper on the countertop. Roll the fondant to ¼ inch thick. To give the snakeskin a textured look, use scissors to cut the webbed onion or citrus bag so it lies flat in one large piece. Place the material over the fondant, place a piece of parchment over it, and roll a rolling pin over it just once.

Place the first Bundt cake on a cake plate (or whatever you would like to serve it on). Use an offset spatula or a table knife to spread the buttercream frosting thinly around the cake, creating a crumb coat where the fondant will be placed. Arrange the fondant around the cake, ensuring the cake is completely covered in fondant. Repeat these steps for the second Bundt cake. Place the other Bundt cake on top of the first cake so they are stacked on one another.

Cover the crispy rice cereal-and-marshmallow head and tail in frosting, and then cover with fondant and arrange them around the snake. Place the neck

inside the opening of the Bundt cakes, pressing it to the bottom to secure it to the baking sheet. Place the tail on the back side of the Bundt cakes, bringing it around to the front the way a coiled snake's tail would rest.

Use your fingers to roll the black cake icing fondant into ¼-inch-round eyes. Use your fingers to roll the yellow cake icing fondant into slightly smaller flat circles to fit over the black eyes. Roll a ¼-inch strip of black cake icing fondant. Place the yellow fondant circle on the black fondant circle and the black strip in the center of the yellow circle, running vertically through the center of the yellow eye. Arrange the fondant eyes on the snake, pressing hard to adhere them fully.

Use a rolling pin to flatten the red cake icing fondant to make the tongue of the snake. Use a paring knife to cut a V shape into the front of the tongue. Place the tongue in the front of the head on top of the mouth. Press hard to secure the fondant together.

Spray the cake with gold cake-decorating luster spray. Use your thumb to smudge the bronze luster dust in large, uneven, and unmatching spots on the snake. With your finger or a small paintbrush, draw a black border around each of the bronze spots on the snake with the black cookie-decorating icing.

MR H POTTER
The Cupboard under the Stairs,
4 Privet Drive,
Little Whinging
SURREY.
HAPPEE
BIRTHDAE
HARRY

CHOCOLATE BIRTHDAE CAKE

YIELD: 12 to 14 servings

One of the sweetest moments in *Harry Potter and the Sorcerer's Stone* is when Hagrid presents Harry with a crumpled cake box for his eleventh birthday. "Baked it meself, words an' all," Hagrid says. "Well, it's not ev'ry day yer young man turns 'leven now is it."

The cake, a chocolate treat covered in bright pink frosting with "Happee Birthdae Harry" written on it, is a symbol of Hagrid's care and kindness, as he takes Harry under his wing. This recipe guides you through creating a classic chocolate cake and decorating it just like Hagrid's. Make this for a fun movie night or to give to someone special to show you care.

- ½ cup plus 1 tablespoon unsalted butter, softened and divided
- 2 cups light brown sugar
- 2 eggs, separated
- 6 teaspoons cocoa powder
- ½ cup boiling water
- 1 teaspoon ground cinnamon
- ½ teaspoon freshly grated nutmeg
- ½ teaspoon ground ginger
- 2¼ cups all-purpose flour
- 1 teaspoon baking soda
- ½ teaspoon baking powder
- ½ teaspoon salt
- ½ cup whole milk
- 1 vanilla bean pod
- 1 recipe Buttercream Frosting (page 149)
- 3 to 5 drops green gel food coloring
- 3 to 5 drops pink gel food coloring

Preheat the oven to 350°F. Grease a 9-inch round cake pan with 1 tablespoon of butter.

In the bowl of a stand mixer, or in a large mixing bowl with a handheld mixer, cream the remaining ½ cup of butter and the light brown sugar on medium speed until light and fluffy, 6 to 7 minutes. Add the egg yolks and beat to combine.

In a separate small bowl, beat the egg whites until they become frothy. In another small bowl, mix the cocoa and boiling water until dissolved, then add it to the egg whites along with the cinnamon, nutmeg, and ginger. Stir to combine.

In another mixing bowl, whisk together the flour, baking soda, baking powder, and salt. Add it to the butter mixture in three portions, alternating with the milk. Use a paring knife to cut the vanilla pod and scrape the seeds into the cake batter. Fold in the egg whites.

Pour the cake batter into the prepared cake pan and bake until a toothpick inserted into the center comes out clean, 35 to 40 minutes. Set the cake on a cooling rack.

Add green food coloring to ½ cup of buttercream frosting in a bowl to make green frosting. Add pink food coloring to 1½ cups of buttercream frosting.

To ASSEMBLE:

When the cake is cooled, use an offset spatula or table knife to cover it in the pink frosting. Use a cake-decorating bag and tip to write on the cake in green frosting.

"I'VE GOT SOMETHING FOR YEH. 'FRAID I MIGHT'VE SAT ON IT AT SOME POINT, BUT I IMAGINE IT'LL TASTE FINE JUST THE SAME."

—Rubeus Hagrid, *Harry Potter and the Sorcerer's Stone*

CAULDRON CANELÉS

YIELD: 12 servings

These canelés are a whimsical twist on the beloved Cauldron Cakes from the Harry Potter films. Traditionally, canelés are small French pastries with a rum-and-vanilla-infused custard center, surrounded by a caramelized, dark crust. Here, homemade hard candy flames in shades of red, yellow, and orange crown the cakes, evoking the fiery essence of a bubbling cauldron. In the wizarding world, Cauldron Cakes are a popular treat on the Hogwarts Express, often purchased from the trolley by Harry and his friends.

CANELÉS:

- ½ vanilla bean pod
- 3 cups milk
- 15 tablespoons butter, divided
- 1 cup granulated sugar
- ⅔ cup all-purpose flour
- 2 large eggs
- 1 large egg yolk
- 3 tablespoons rum
- 1 tablespoon chopped fresh or dried lavender buds
- ⅓ cup beeswax, finely chopped

CANDY FLAMES:

- Sorcerer's Stone Candies (page 34)
- 5 drops red liquid food coloring
- 5 drops orange liquid food coloring
- 5 drops yellow liquid food coloring

SPECIALTY TOOLS

- Canelé molds
- Pastry brush
- Candy thermometer

"ANYTHING SWEET FOR YOU, DEAR?"

—The Trolley Witch, *Harry Potter and the Goblet of Fire*

To MAKE THE CANELÉS:

Use a paring knife to open the vanilla bean pod and scrape the vanilla from the pod. Discard the pod.

In a small saucepan over high heat, combine the milk and vanilla. Bring to a boil, then remove from heat. Add 3 tablespoons of butter and stir to combine. Set aside to cool.

In a large mixing bowl, use a wire whisk to whisk together the sugar and flour.

In a separate large mixing bowl, use a wire whisk to whisk together the two eggs, egg yolk, and rum. Next, whisk the egg mixture into the sugar-and-flour mixture, then whisk in the milk mixture. Add the lavender buds (saving a few for garnish) and stir into the batter. Pour the batter into an airtight container and refrigerate overnight.

In a small saucepan over low heat, melt the beeswax and the remaining 12 tablespoons of butter. Stir the wax and butter together while the mixture heats. Once it is well blended, remove from heat. Using a pastry brush, brush the insides of the canelé molds with the mixture.

Remove the batter from the refrigerator at least 1 hour before baking.

Preheat the oven to 425°F.

Pour the batter into the molds. Fill each mold only two-thirds full to create mini canelés.

Bake until the canelés are dark brown, about 1 hour. Remove the molds from the oven and remove each canelé from its mold. Set them upright on a cooling rack to cool.

These canelés can be stored in an airtight container at room temperature for 2 to 3 days.

QIZILBASH
CAULDRON
CAKES
Free Wizard and Witches Cards Inside!

"WE'LL TAKE THE LOT!"

—Harry Potter, *Harry Potter and the Sorcerer's Stone*

TO MAKE THE CANDY FLAMES:

Line two baking sheets with parchment paper.

Follow the Sorcerer's Stone Candies recipe. Before adding the food coloring, separate the mixture into three heatproof containers and blend five drops of food coloring into each pan: red, yellow, and orange.

Using a separate small spoon for each color, quickly drizzle each of the sugar mixtures onto the baking sheets. Spread the sugar mixture to make pieces in a variety of widths and lengths.

Let the sugar flames rest until they become hardened enough to stand upright on their own, 6 to 8 minutes. Store between layers of parchment in airtight containers until you are ready to serve.

Push two or three pieces of the candy flames into the top of each of the canelés and serve each guest a canelé on a dessert plate.

OPTIONAL: Serve the canelés with Cornelius Fudge Sauce (page 88).

GOLDEN SNITCH CUPCAKES

YIELD: 24 to 28 cupcakes

In Quidditch, the Seeker's job is to find and catch the Golden Snitch, and that's exactly what Harry Potter excels at in his first flying lesson at Hogwarts. During the lesson, Harry impresses Professor McGonagall by catching Neville's Remembrall after Draco Malfoy taunts him. Soon after, Harry is made Seeker for the Gryffindor Quidditch team. These Golden Snitch cupcakes celebrate Harry's Quidditch skills and the iconic Golden Snitch. Made from malt balls and edible wafer paper, these cupcakes are the perfect tribute to the most beloved game in the wizarding world and the skilled Seeker Harry becomes during his years at Hogwarts.

CUPCAKES:

- 1 cup (2 sticks) butter, plus 2 tablespoons for greasing (optional), softened
- 2 cups granulated sugar
- 4 eggs, room temperature
- 3 cups all-purpose flour
- 1 tablespoon baking powder
- 1 cup milk, room temperature
- 2 teaspoons vanilla extract
- 1 recipe Buttercream Frosting (page 149)

MALTED MILK BALL SNITCHES:

- 2 or 3 sheets edible wafer paper
- ½ cup nonpareils
- 1 tablespoon gold luster dust
- 24 to 28 jumbo malt balls in milk or dark chocolate

To MAKE THE CUPCAKES:

Preheat the oven to 350°F.

Butter the cavities of a 12-cup cupcake pan with 2 tablespoons of butter, making sure the bottoms and sides are completely covered, or use gold cupcake liners.

In a large bowl with a handheld mixer at medium speed, beat the remaining 1 cup of butter and the sugar together until the mixture becomes light and fluffy, about 4 minutes.

Add the eggs, one at a time, to the mixture. After each egg is added, beat until combined well.

Place the flour and baking powder in a separate medium bowl and use a spoon to stir them together.

Add one-third of the flour mixture to the butter mixture, followed by one-third of the milk; repeat two more times until both are completely added to the butter mixture. After each addition, beat until mixed together well, about 1 minute. Add the vanilla and beat to combine well, about 1 minute.

Fill three-quarters of each cavity in the cupcake tin with the batter.

Bake the cupcakes in the oven until each one becomes browned on top and around the edges and starts to pull away from the edges of the pan. They are baked through when a knife or toothpick comes out clean when inserted into the center of one of them, about 45 minutes.

Remove the cupcakes from the oven and set them aside to cool, about 1 hour.

"HAVE YOU HEARD? HARRY POTTER'S THE NEW GRYFFINDOR SEEKER! I ALWAYS KNEW HE'D DO WELL."

—Nearly Headless Nick, *Harry Potter and the Sorcerer's Stone*

FIXTURES
RESULT

To MAKE THE MALTED MILK BALL SNITCHES:

Cut out a pair of Snitch wings from the wafer paper for each cupcake. Leave a long-pointed bit at the end of each wing to insert into the cupcake, and make small snips all along the length of each wing to create its "feathers." For ease, keep the lefts and rights separate.

Fill a small sealable container with the nonpareils and add the luster dust. Seal the container and give it a good shake to evenly distribute the luster dust. Add the wings, one or two at a time, and gently shake to cover with gold. Once all the wings have been coated, coat each of the malt balls in the same way. Set these pieces aside until ready to assemble.

To ASSEMBLE:

When the cupcakes have cooled, use an offset spatula to spread frosting on top of each cupcake, or pipe the frosting on with a large star tip.

Place a malted milk ball Snitch in the center on top of each of the cupcakes.

Set a pair of wings on either side of each of the malted milk ball Snitches. Gently press the wings into the frosting to secure them.

FLURRY OF LETTERS CAKE

YIELD: 16 servings

In *Harry Potter and the Sorcerer's Stone*, Vernon Dursley frantically destroys each Hogwarts acceptance letter addressed to Harry, but one day, a flurry of letters overwhelms him. Dudley exclaims, "Daddy's gone mad, hasn't he?!" as the magical messages flood in. Atop this cream cheese and vanilla cake are perched a flock of owl cookies, surrounded by edible envelopes sealed with red icing. The seals, embossed with the letter *H* for Hogwarts, decorate the cake, with one envelope even displaying Harry Potter's address. The sweet vanilla buttercream frosting and attention to detail make this cake a memorable centerpiece for any celebration.

CAKE:

- 2¼ cups plus 4 tablespoons butter, softened and divided
- 12 ounces cream cheese, softened
- 4½ cups granulated sugar
- 2 vanilla bean pods or 2 teaspoons vanilla paste
- 9 large eggs, room temperature
- 4½ cups all-purpose flour
- 4½ teaspoons baking powder
- ¼ teaspoon sea salt

BUTTERCREAM FROSTING:

- 1½ cups egg whites
- 3 cups granulated sugar
- 2 pounds (8 sticks) salted butter, softened, cut into 1-tablespoon chunks
- 2 teaspoons vanilla

OWL COOKIES:

- ¾ cup salted butter, softened
- 4 ounces cream cheese, softened
- ¾ cup light brown sugar, firmly packed
- 1 egg
- 1 teaspoon vanilla
- 3 cups all-purpose flour

ROYAL ICING:

- 4 cups powdered sugar, sifted
- 3 tablespoons meringue powder
- 6 tablespoons water
- 2 or 3 drops each of black, yellow, copper, brown, and orange food coloring

ASSEMBLY:

- Two 8½-by-11-inch sheets of edible wafer paper, .33 mm thick
- 1 cup red candy melts
- 3 cups strawberry jam
- 2 pretzel rods (optional)

SPECIALTY TOOLS

- Owl-shaped cookie cutters
- 1 black edible-ink pen
- Letter *H* wax seal stamp for letters, 2.5 centimeters, or Hogwarts crest seal
- 8- and 6-inch cake pans
- 8- and 6-inch cake rounds (optional)
- Pastry bags and writing tips

TO MAKE THE CAKE:

Preheat the oven to 350°F.

Cut a parchment round to fit the bottom of each cake pan. You will need three 8-inch layers and three 6-inch layers. Grease the sides of each cake pan with the 4 tablespoons of butter.

In the bowl of a stand mixer, or in a large bowl with a handheld mixer, cream the remaining butter and cream cheese on high speed for 1 to 2 minutes.

PRIVET DRIVE
MR. H. POTTER
The Cupboard under the Stairs,
4, Privet Drive,
Little Whinging,
SURREY

Continue beating while slowly adding the sugar. Beat on high for 1 to 2 minutes.

Use a paring knife to open the vanilla bean pods and scrape the insides. Add the vanilla to the mixer and beat for another minute.

Reduce the speed to low and add the eggs, one at a time. Add flour, baking powder, and sea salt and mix at medium speed just until well combined.

Each 8-inch layer will need 3 cups of batter, and each 6-inch layer will need 1¼ cups of batter. Bake in the oven until a toothpick comes out of the center clean, 30 to 35 minutes for the 8-inch cakes and 25 to 30 minutes for the 6-inch cakes.

Remove the cakes and set them on cooling racks to cool in the pans for 15 minutes. Gently loosen the edges with an offset spatula and release them from the pans to finish cooling on the cooling racks. Do not frost until completely cool. The cakes can be made ahead, wrapped in plastic wrap, and refrigerated for up to 3 days or frozen for up to 2 weeks.

To MAKE THE BUTTERCREAM FROSTING:

Place a heatproof measuring cup or bowl inside a saucepan. Fill the saucepan with water until the water level reaches halfway up the cup. Remove the measuring cup and turn the heat to medium. Bring the water to a simmer.

In the measuring cup, combine the egg whites and sugar and whisk until blended. Place the measuring cup into the simmering water and cook, stirring constantly, until the sugar is completely dissolved and the mixture is hot.

With an oven mitt, carefully remove the measuring cup containing the egg-sugar mixture from the saucepan and transfer the mixture to the bowl of a stand mixer fitted with a whisk attachment. Whisk the egg-sugar mixture on high until it is completely cool, up to 7 to 10 minutes. The mixture should be opaque and white, with elastic ribbons flowing from the beater—a loose, sticky meringue.

Add the softened butter to the meringue, one piece at a time, with the mixer on low, until all the butter is incorporated.

Add the vanilla, turn up the mixer to medium, and mix until smooth, 1 to 2 minutes more. Set aside.

To MAKE THE OWL COOKIES:

In a large bowl, beat together the butter, cream cheese, and sugar until light and fluffy. Add the egg and vanilla and beat again until well combined. Add the flour, 1 cup at a time, mixing on low and then mixing by hand with the last cup.

Split the dough in half, form into disks, wrap in parchment paper, and chill for at least 1 hour. Toward the end of the hour, preheat the oven to 375°F.

After chilling the dough, work with one half at a time on a lightly floured surface. Roll out each disk to ⅛ inch thick and cut out as many owls as you can with the cookie cutters. Transfer the cookies to a baking sheet, rewrap the scraps, and chill both the scraps and the cookies while working with the second disk. If desired, cut out a long rectangle to create the Privet Drive sign.

Repeat with the second disk and make sure the cookies chill for at least 10 minutes before baking. Bake for 9 to 11 minutes or until just starting to brown at the edges. Allow to cool on a wire rack.

To MAKE THE ROYAL ICING:

In the bowl of a stand mixer fitted with the whisk attachment, combine the powdered sugar, meringue powder, and water. Whisk on low speed for 7 to 10 minutes or until the icing holds stiff peaks. (If using a hand mixer, whisk on high speed for 10 to 12 minutes.)

Divide the icing into five small bowls and use the food coloring to create your desired colors. Transfer the icing to pastry bags fitted with writing tips. Decorate the owls to match the ones that appear in the scene, all English owl breeds, or create your own.

Allow the cookies to dry completely, at least 3 hours, before serving, packaging, or storing. Store in an airtight container between layers of parchment paper or place each cookie in a cellophane bag for gifting.

To MAKE THE ENVELOPES AND SEALS:

Use scissors to cut out multiple letter sizes, from $1\frac{1}{2}$ inches by $2\frac{1}{2}$ inches to $2\frac{1}{2}$ inches by $3\frac{1}{2}$ inches, for a total of 12 to 15 letters from pieces of edible paper. Use a black edible-ink pen to draw lines where the flap of an envelope would be located.

Place the candy melts in a small bowl and melt them in the microwave. Quickly, before the melted candy hardens, use a $\frac{1}{4}$-teaspoon measuring spoon to place small amounts onto parchment paper to cool slightly. When they are soft but not yet hardened, press the letter stamp firmly into each of the candy circles and let sit until the candy is firm and the stamp easily pulls away. Having a bowl of ice water and a paper towel to cool down the stamp and then wipe away any water can speed up this process. Store the candy seals in an airtight container until ready to attach to the letters. When ready to attach, melt the remaining candy melts and use a small dot to attach each seal to a letter.

On another piece of edible paper, use a black edible-ink pen to write Harry Potter's address:

Mr. H. Potter
The Cupboard Under the Stairs
4. Privet Drive
Little Whinging
SURREY

To ASSEMBLE THE CAKE:

On a cake plate or board, place a small dollop of frosting and center an 8-inch layer of cake over it. Frost the top with a thin layer a frosting, pushing the bulk of it toward the edges to create a small wall. Fill the center of the cake by spreading a scant cup of jam over the layer of frosting. Repeat with the second layer and top with the final layer. Frost the entire cake with a thin crumb coat and refrigerate while you work on the 6-inch tier.

If using, cut the 6-inch cake round so that it is slightly small then the 6-inch cake. Place a dollop of frosting on the cake round and center a layer of cake over it. Frost the top with a thin layer of frosting, creating a low wall like you did with the 8-inch cakes. Fill the center with $\frac{1}{2}$ cup of jam and repeat with the second layer. Place the third layer on top

and crumb-coat the entire cake. Refrigerate for at least 20 minutes before doing the final assembly.

Once both cakes have been completely frosted and you are ready to assemble, place the 6-inch tier on the 8-inch one, setting it back a little to make space in front for letters and owls.

If using the Privet Drive sign, use royal icing to attach the pretzel rods to the back of the sign and press them gently into the cake.

Arrange the owls and envelopes around the cake. Press them into the frosting to secure them. Leave the corners of the envelopes free to give the appearance of the flurry of envelopes Harry receives.

GRYFFINDOR SCARF CAKE

YIELD: 12 servings

Traditionally made with almond flour and flavored with vanilla and almond extracts, English Battenberg cake features a distinctive four-square checkerboard pattern. This version, known as the Gryffindor Scarf Cake, showcases scarlet and gold squares squares that evoke the iconic Gryffindor house scarf, proudly worn by Harry Potter and his fellow Gryffindors. The vibrant cake layers sandwich bright, zesty orange marmalade, adding a burst of citrus flavor, and are wrapped in a smooth, thin layer of marzipan for a sweet, almond finish. When sliced, the bold, contrasting colors reveal a striking pattern reminiscent of Hogwarts house scarves, making it both a visually captivating and delicious treat.

- 1 cup all-purpose flour
- ½ cup almond flour
- ¾ cup butter, softened
- 1 cup granulated sugar
- 1 teaspoon baking powder
- ½ teaspoon pink Himalayan sea salt
- 3 large eggs, room temperature
- 1 teaspoon almond extract
- ⅓ cup whole milk
- 1 vanilla bean pod
- 4 drops yellow food coloring
- 12 drops red food coloring
- 3 drops blue food coloring
- 1 cup orange marmalade
- 16 ounces white marzipan

"THE HOUSE OF GODRIC GRYFFINDOR HAS COMMANDED THE RESPECT OF THE WIZARD WORLD FOR NEARLY TEN CENTURIES."

—Professor Minerva McGonagall, *Harry Potter and the Goblet of Fire*

Preheat the oven to 350°F.

Line a 9-by-5-inch loaf pan with parchment paper. Fold aluminum foil to fit in the middle of the loaf pan, dividing the pan lengthwise. Place a piece of parchment paper over the divider.

In the bowl of a stand mixer, or in a large bowl with a handheld mixer on medium speed, beat the flours and butter until well combined, 1 to 2 minutes. Add sugar, baking powder, and sea salt while continuing to beat to combine the ingredients. Add the eggs, one at a time, while continuing to beat the mixture. Beat in the almond extract and milk. Use a paring knife to open and scrape the vanilla bean pod and add the vanilla from inside to the mixture. Discard the pod. Beat constantly until the batter is smooth.

Separate the batter into two bowls. Color the batter in one bowl yellow with the yellow food coloring, and the batter in the other bowl burgundy with the red and blue food coloring.

Pour the burgundy batter into one side of the loaf pan, and pour the yellow batter into the other side of the pan.

Place the cake in the oven and bake until a toothpick inserted in the middle comes out clean, 35 to 40 minutes. Remove the cake from the oven and set aside to cool.

When the cake is cool, use a serrated knife to cut both sides (yellow and burgundy) horizontally, creating 4 rectangular strips. You should now have two strips of yellow cake and two strips of burgundy cake. Use the knife to carefully trim off the uneven parts of the cake, making sure not to remove too much.

On a cake plate, place one yellow strip of cake next to a burgundy strip of cake. Use a table knife to spread a thin layer of marmalade on top of the cake layer. Next, stack the remaining burgundy strip of cake on top of the yellow cake that is already on the

HOGWARTS

GRYF

plate, and the remaining yellow strip of cake on the burgundy strip of cake, creating a checkered pattern. Use a table knife to spread a thick layer of marmalade around the whole cake.

With a rolling pin, roll out the white marzipan to ¼ inch thick in the shape of a rectangle. Place the marzipan over the cake and press it into the sides. Use a paring knife or a table knife to trim the excess marizipan around the bottom edge and slice triangle sections out of the corners to allow the marzipan to fit snugly around the cake.

Use a serrated knife to slice the cake open to reveal the charming pattern inside.

"EXCELLENT, TEN POINTS TO GRYFFINDOR!"

—Professor Pomona Sprout,
Harry Potter and the Chamber of Secrets

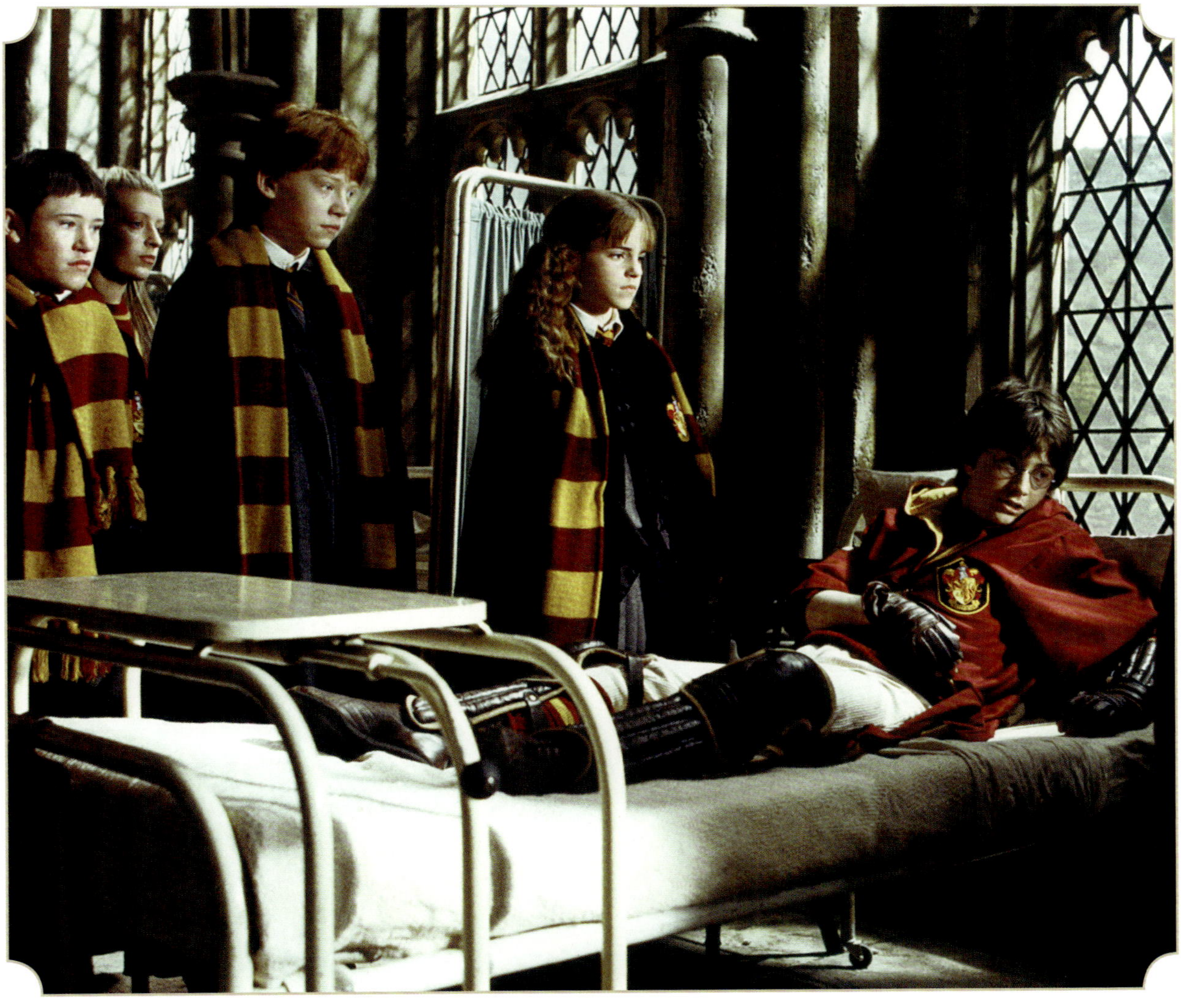

CHAPTER 4

PIES, TARTS & SWEET SAUCES

CORNELIUS FUDGE SAUCE

YIELD: 4 servings

Rich, velvety, and impossible to resist, this classic fudge sauce is named after the Minister of Magic himself, Cornelius Fudge, whose tenure was marked by denial, ambition, and eventual downfall. But unlike its namesake, this sauce won't disappoint. It is perfect for drizzling over cakes, profiteroles, ice cream, or anything that could use a touch of chocolate decadence. Fudge's refusal to face the truth led to his undoing, but you can trust this recipe to deliver every time. Whether you're hosting a Triwizard Tournament feast or just treating yourself, this luscious fudge sauce is a magical addition to any dessert table—no Ministry approval required.

4 tablespoons (½ stick) butter
¼ cup whipping cream
½ cup granulated sugar
¼ cup cocoa powder

"IN TIMES LIKE THESE, THE WIZARD WORLD LOOKS TO ITS LEADERS FOR STRENGTH . . . I WILL NOT BE SEEN AS A COWARD!"

—Cornelius Fudge, *Harry Potter and the Goblet of Fire*

In a medium saucepan over medium-low heat, melt the butter. Once melted, use a wire whisk to whisk in the cream. Whisk in the sugar and cocoa powder. Stir with the whisk until the sugar and cocoa powder dissolve. Continue to simmer, stirring occasionally, until the sauce thickens, 2 to 3 minutes.

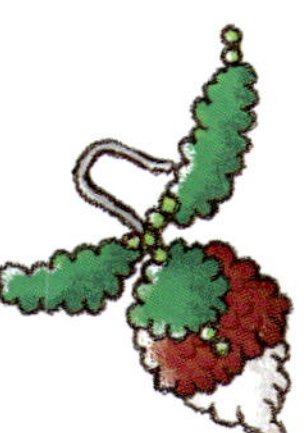

LUNA LOVEGOOD SWEET RADISH SAUCE

YIELD: 24 servings

Vibrant and completely unexpected, this sweet radish sauce is as memorable as Luna Lovegood's signature Dirigible Plum earrings, which are often mistaken for radishes. Its unique, tangy-sweet flavor adds a delightful twist when drizzled over pies, cakes, or plump slices of fruit. Try it atop ice cream for a zesty contrast or freeze it into refreshing ice pops (see Romilda's Romance Fizz, page 117). Inspired by Luna's whimsical charm and the curious radish-like Dirigible Plums growing near her home, this sauce celebrates her knack for seeing beauty in the unusual. Just as Luna stood out at Hogwarts with her bold spirit and unwavering loyalty, this sauce leaves a lasting impression—quirky, bright, and wonderfully one of a kind.

20 small radishes
1 cup granulated sugar
¼ cup water

"UNFORTUNATELY, ALL MY SHOES HAVE MYSTERIOUSLY DISAPPEARED. I SUSPECT NARGLES ARE BEHIND IT."

—Luna Lovegood, *Harry Potter and the Order of the Phoenix*

Clean and trim the radishes. Cut the radishes into ½-inch pieces.

In a food processor, pulse the radishes two or three times, until they become shredded like confetti. This will make about 1 cup of shredded radishes.

In a medium saucepan, combine the radishes, sugar, and water. Bring to a boil, stirring occasionally. Reduce the heat and simmer until thickened and the radishes are tender, 2 to 3 minutes.

Remove the sauce from the heat and set aside to let cool.

HOUSE SYRUPS

YIELD: About 1 cup of each syrup

Each Hogwarts house comes with its own set of characteristics and colors. From Gryffindor's bravery and Hufflepuff's loyalty to Slytherin's ambition and Ravenclaw's wisdom, each house brings out the best in its inhabitants. Each of these syrups represents the houses and their main colors, and despite the difference in flavors, they are all sweet treats used to top some of your favorite desserts and, of course, are best enjoyed with friends. Which house do you belong to?

SLYTHERIN SYRUP

1 cup sugar
½ cup water
1 cup loosely packed basil leaves

In a small saucepan over medium-high heat, combine the sugar and water. Bring to a boil, stirring occasionally, until all the sugar is dissolved. Pour into a blender container and allow to cool for 15 minutes.

Add the basil leaves to the blender and blend on high or extract for 15 to 30 seconds. Allow to steep for 15 minutes before running through a fine-mesh strainer, discarding the solids, and refrigerating the syrup until needed.

NOTE: Basil makes a wonderful syrup that pairs well with the other houses, but the same method will also work with mint, although with a less vibrant green.

RAVENCLAW SYRUP

3-inch piece ginger
1 cup sugar
½ cup water
2 tablespoons butterfly pea flowers

Peel the ginger and slice it into thick slices, smashing it a little with the back of the knife.

In a small saucepan over medium-high heat, combine the ginger, sugar, and water. Bring to a boil, stirring occasionally, until the sugar is dissolved. Remove from the heat and let steep for 10 minutes.

After 10 minutes, add the butterfly pea flowers and steep another 15 to 20 minutes or until the desired blue is reached.

Strain through a fine-mesh strainer, discarding the solids, and refrigerating the syrup until needed.

NOTE: Dried butterfly pea flowers can be purchased online or in specialty stores or found in some teas.

GRYFFINDOR SYRUP

½ cup fresh raspberries
1 cup granulated sugar
½ cup water

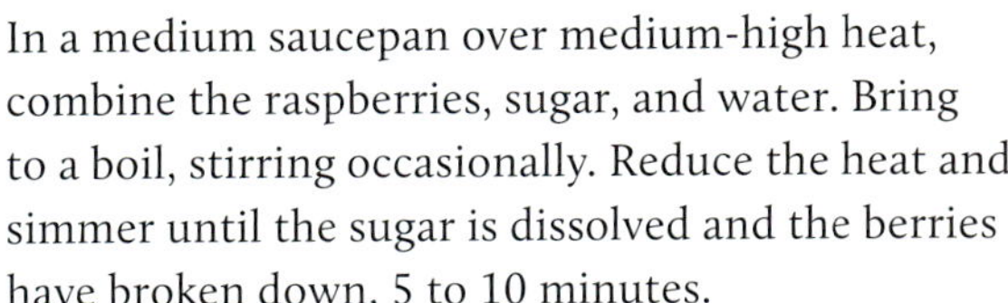

In a medium saucepan over medium-high heat, combine the raspberries, sugar, and water. Bring to a boil, stirring occasionally. Reduce the heat and simmer until the sugar is dissolved and the berries have broken down, 5 to 10 minutes.

Remove the sauce from the heat. Run the sauce through a fine-mesh strainer, discarding the solids and refrigerating the syrup until needed.

HUFFLEPUFF SYRUP

1 tablespoon lemon zest (about 2 lemons)
2 tablespoons lemon juice
¼ teaspoon turmeric, for color (optional)
1 cup sugar
½ cup water

In a small saucepan over medium-high heat, combine the lemon zest, lemon juice, turmeric (if using), sugar, and water. Bring to a boil, stirring occasionally, until the sugar is dissolved. Remove from the heat and let steep for 15 minutes. Pour through a fine-mesh strainer, discarding the solids, and refrigerating the syrup until needed.

Viktor Krum

KRUM TRIWIZARD TIKVENIK

YIELD: 14 to 16 servings

A beloved Bulgarian dessert, tikvenik is a coiled pumpkin strudel made with crisp phyllo pastry and a spiced pumpkin filling flavored with cinnamon, nutmeg, and cardamom. This flaky treat ties perfectly to Viktor Krum, the famed Bulgarian Seeker introduced in *Harry Potter and the Goblet of Fire*. At just eighteen, Krum was already a Quidditch star, playing in the World Cup final before arriving at Hogwarts as Durmstrang's champion in the Triwizard Tournament. Bulgaria didn't win the Cup, but Krum's skill was undeniable—just like the appeal of this warm, aromatic pastry. Serve tikvenik dusted with powdered sugar or a dollop of Whipped Cream (page 148) for a dessert that's as bold and memorable as Durmstrang's finest wizard.

STRUDEL:

1 package frozen phyllo dough

Cooking spray

4 cups canned puréed pumpkin

⅓ cup light brown sugar

2 teaspoons ground cinnamon

2 teaspoons freshly grated or ground nutmeg

2 teaspoons ground cardamom

½ cup butter, melted

1 cup chopped walnuts

TOPPING:

3 tablespoons granulated sugar

1 tablespoon ground cinnamon

1 tablespoon powdered sugar

1 recipe Whipped Cream (page 148)

SPECIALTY TOOLS

Pastry brush

Preheat the oven to 350°F.

Remove the phyllo dough from the freezer 45 minutes before using. Spray cooking spray in a 9-inch round tart pan.

In a large bowl, mix the pumpkin, brown sugar, cinnamon, nutmeg, and cardamom.

Spread two sheets of phyllo dough out on the countertop. Use a pastry brush to lightly coat the dough with melted butter. Use a spoon to place a spoonful of pumpkin mixture along the edge of the dough on one of the short ends. Roll the end toward the middle, giving it one turn to wrap the pumpkin mixture. Sprinkle with the walnuts and finish rolling until the dough is in a cylindrical shape. Repeat this process five more times, until you have enough rolls to coil in the pie plate to completely fill it.

Brush the remaining butter on the top. In a small bowl, combine the granulated sugar and cinnamon for the topping and sprinkle it all around on the top of the strudel.

Place the strudel in the oven and bake until it is lightly golden brown and crispy all around, 30 to 35 minutes.

Remove the strudel from the oven and set aside to cool.

When the strudel has cooled, place the powdered sugar in a sifter and shake the sugar onto the tikvenik.

Serve the strudel warm with whipped cream.

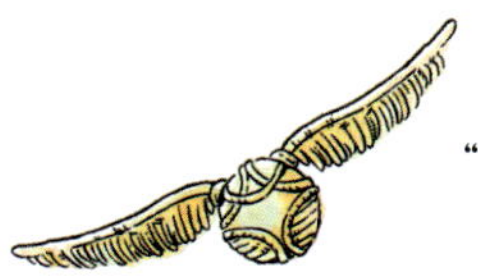

"THAT, SIS, IS THE BEST SEEKER IN THE WORLD."

—Fred Weasley, *Harry Potter and the Goblet of Fire*

MOLLY WEASLEY MINCE PIE

YIELD: 8 to 12 servings

Mince pies are a beloved British holiday treat, often appearing at Christmas feasts. Harry and Ginny even munch on them during Christmas at The Burrow in *Harry Potter and the Half-Blood Prince*. These pies are typically filled with a spiced mixture of dried fruits such as raisins, golden raisins, dried cranberries, and diced apple, along with almonds, spices, citrus zest, and brandy. For a delightful balance, serve these rich pies with a scoop of Frozen Butterscotch (see page 143) or a heaping spoonful of Whipped Cream (page 148). You can make them in either a 9-inch tart pan or mini tart pans for a festive presentation.

- 1 recipe Piecrust (page 148)
- 1 cup granulated sugar
- ½ cup butter
- ¼ cup raisins
- ¼ cup golden raisins
- ¼ cup dried cranberries
- 1 Honeycrisp apple, cored and diced with the skin on
- ¼ cup slivered almonds
- Zest of 1 orange
- Zest of 1 lemon
- ¼ teaspoon freshly grated nutmeg
- ¼ teaspoon ground cinnamon
- 1 cup peach brandy

SPECIALTY TOOLS

Shallow 9-inch pie plate

Follow the piecrust directions to make one piecrust.

If desired, use the dough scraps from the piecrust recipe to cut out small shapes to decorate the pie, such as leaves or apples.

While the crust is baking, in a saucepan over medium-low heat, combine the sugar, butter, raisins, cranberries, and apple. Stir until the butter melts completely. Add the almonds, orange and lemon zest, nutmeg, and cinnamon. Stir to combine well. Add the brandy. Continue to simmer, stirring occasionally, until the brandy blends completely into the mixture and the mixture thickens, 10 to 15 minutes.

Remove the piecrust from the oven when it is golden brown and reduce the heat to 350°F. Pour the pie filling into the piecrust. Sprinkle the topping for the pie on top. Place the pie in the oven for 50 minutes.

Remove the pie from the oven and set aside to cool before serving.

WEASLEY & WEASLEY PRODUCTS
presents
THE
SKIVING SNACKBOX
E OF SWEETS
AKE YOU ILL!!!
SERIOUSLY ILL, JUST ILL ENOUGH
O GET YOU OUT OF TROUBLE...
SKIVING SNACKBOX
WIZARD WHEEZES
un for everyone!
QUALI
WEASL
GOODS

WEASLEY TWINS VANILLA CUSTARD PIE

YIELD: 8 to 12 servings

This vanilla custard pie is a playful twist on the Weasley twins' famous self-propelling custard pie from their joke shop, Weasleys' Wizard Wheezes. Though their pie was designed to land in someone's face, this version is a delicious dessert featuring a smooth, velvety vanilla custard filling, topped with fluffy whipped cream. The light and creamy pie blends humor with flavor, making it a whimsical yet satisfying treat that perfectly embodies the mischievous spirit of the Weasley twins' magical inventions.

PIECRUST:

- ½ recipe Piecrust (page 148)
- 1 or 2 tablespoons orange sanding sugar (optional)
- 1 or 2 tablespoons purple sanding sugar (optional)

CUSTARD PIE FILLING:

- 3 tablespoons cornstarch
- 3 cups whole milk, divided
- ¼ teaspoon pink Himalayan sea salt
- 1 cup sugar
- 3 egg yolks
- 1 vanilla bean pod
- 1 tablespoon butter, softened
- 1 recipe Whipped Cream (page 148)

To MAKE THE PIECRUST:

Follow the recipe for piecrust to make the pie dough. If desired, use the dough scraps to cut a *W* and star for the Weasley logo, sprinkle it with orange and purple sanding sugar, and bake at 425°F for 8 to 10 minutes or until crisp.

To MAKE THE CUSTARD PUDDING PIE FILLING:

In a large mixing bowl, whisk the cornstarch and ¼ cup of milk.

In a medium saucepan over medium heat, whisk together the remaining 2¾ cups of milk, sea salt, and sugar. Cook, stirring occasionally, until there is steam and then remove from heat.

In a medium bowl, whisk the egg yolks. Pour ½ cup of the steamed milk into the egg yolks and stir constantly. Slowly pour the egg mixture and the cornstarch mixture back into the saucepan and simmer, whisking constantly, until the mixture thickens.

Use a paring knife to open the vanilla bean pod and scrape the vanilla from the pod. Discard the pod. Set the vanilla from the pod on a medium plate on the countertop.

Remove the pudding from the heat; stir in the butter and the vanilla that was scraped from the pod.

When the piecrust is cool enough, fill it with the custard pie filling.

To ASSEMBLE:

Use an offset spatula or a table knife to spread whipped cream all around the top of the pie. Decorate with the *W* and star.

PROFESSOR SPROUT ROSEMARY-SCENTED LEMON PIE

YIELD: 8 servings

Professor Sprout's greenhouse was home to all kinds of magical plants. In *Harry Potter and the Chamber of Secrets*, she welcomes second-year students into Greenhouse Three, ready to teach them about the wonders—and dangers—of Herbology. This bright and zesty lemon pie pays homage to her expertise, with a touch of rosemary to add an earthy depth to the classic tart-sweet curd. Topped with Whipped Cream (page 148), this pie strikes a delicious balance of flavors. Just as Professor Sprout nurtured her magical plants with care, this pie comes together with simple ingredients that shine, making it a refreshing and flavorful dessert worthy of any feast.

PIECRUST:

1 frozen piecrust or 1 recipe Piecrust (page 148)

PIE FILLING:

1½ cups sugar

¼ cup cornstarch

1½ cups water

4 egg yolks

2 tablespoons lemon juice

Zest of 2 large lemons

4 rosemary sprigs, divided

2 tablespoons unsalted butter

1 recipe Whipped Cream (page 148)

½ cup fresh raspberries

TO MAKE THE PIECRUST:

Preheat the oven to 350°F.

If using a frozen piecrust, remove the piecrust from the freezer 45 minutes before using. With a rolling pin, roll out the piecrust. Lay the dough in a 9-inch round pie plate and use your fingers to flute the edges of the dough all around the rim of the pie plate. With a fork to poke air holes in the bottom and sides of the piecrust, 1 inch apart.

Bake the crust in the oven until lightly brown, 8 to 10 minutes.

Remove the crust from the oven and set aside to cool.

TO MAKE THE FILLING:

In a medium saucepan over medium heat, whisk together the sugar, cornstarch, water, eggs, lemon juice, lemon zest, and two rosemary sprigs. Cook, whisking constantly, for 10 to 15 minutes, until the pie filling thickens. Remove from heat and stir in the butter.

Pour the filling into the prebaked crust and bake until the filling is firmly set, 30 to 35 minutes. Remove from the oven and set aside to cool.

TO ASSEMBLE:

When the pie is cool enough, cover the top with whipped cream. Garnish with the remaining rosemary sprigs and the fresh raspberries.

"PLENTY OF POTS TO GO AROUND!"

—Professor Pomona Sprout,
Harry Potter and the Chamber of Secrets

DARK CHOCOLATE DEMENTOR PIE

YIELD: 8 to 10 servings

"Don't put away your wand, Harry. They might come back," warned Mrs. Figg after Harry's harrowing encounter with Dementors in *Harry Potter and the Order of the Phoenix*. Sent from Azkaban to silence him, these Dark creatures forced Harry to cast a powerful Patronus Charm, saving both himself and Dudley from the dreaded Dementor's Kiss—a fate worse than death.

This luxurious chocolate cream pie embodies that dark encounter, topped with clouds of Whipped Cream (page 148) and the shadowy form of a Dementor, drawn with thin strips of black licorice or Treacle Licorice Bites (page 37) and black cookie icing. It's a deliciously dark dessert that's sure to leave an unforgettable impression.

PIECRUST:

1 frozen piecrust

CHOCOLATE PIE FILLING:

⅔ cup granulated sugar

¼ cup cocoa powder

3 tablespoons cornstarch

1 pinch sea salt

2¼ cups whole milk

1 vanilla bean pod

DECORATIVE TOPPING:

1 recipe Whipped Cream (page 148)

8 to 10 drops black food coloring

1 cup store-bought black string licorice or Treacle Licorice Bites (page 37)

"DEMENTORS IN LITTLE WHINGING. WHATEVER NEXT?"

—Arabella Figg, *Harry Potter and the Order of the Phoenix*

TO MAKE THE PIECRUST:

Preheat the oven based on the package directions of the piecrust.

Roll out the frozen piecrust dough and line a 9-inch round pie plate with the dough. Use your fingers to flute the dough around the rim of the pie plate. Use a fork to pierce holes in the base and sides of the piecrust, about 1 inch apart.

Bake the crust in the oven until golden brown, 15 to 18 minutes.

Remove the piecrust from the oven and set it aside to cool.

TO MAKE THE CHOCOLATE PIE FILLING:

In a medium saucepan, combine the sugar, cocoa powder, cornstarch, and sea salt. Use a wire whisk to stir constantly while adding the milk.

Bring the mixture to a boil and then remove from heat. Set the saucepan on the counter.

Use a paring knife to open the vanilla bean pod and scrape the vanilla from the pod. Discard the pod. Add the vanilla from the pod to the pie filling.

When the piecrust is cool enough, fill it with the chocolate cream pie filling.

TO ASSEMBLE:

Use an offset spatula or a table knife to spread whipped cream all around the top of the pie, creating a flat, level surface.

Dye the remaining whipped cream a dark charcoal gray with the black food coloring and place it in a pastry bag with a medium writing tip. Practice drawing the dementor on parchment paper at least once before drawing on the pie. Once you have the dementor on the pie, create depth and definition by adding thin strips of licorice.

Serve each slice of pie with a licorice bite and, of course, a Chocolate Revivor (page 41), which will be needed after a bite of this pie.

GINGERY TREACLE TARTLETS

YIELD: 8 to 10 servings

These Gingery Treacle Tartlets take Harry Potter's favorite dessert—treacle tart—to a new level with a touch of crystallized ginger. A beloved treat in the wizarding and Muggle worlds, treacle tart is traditionally made with shortcrust pastry, golden syrup, and treacle (similar to molasses) and is often served hot with a dollop of clotted cream.

- 4 mini frozen piecrusts or ½ recipe Piecrust (page 148)
- 2 tablespoons yellow sanding sugar (optional)
- 2 to 3 drops black food coloring (optional)
- 1 egg (optional)
- 2 cups breadcrumbs
- ¾ cup golden syrup or corn syrup
- ¼ cup chopped crystallized ginger
- ¼ cup blackstrap molasses or treacle
- Zest and juice of 1 lemon
- 1 recipe Whipped Cream (page 148), for serving

SPECIALTY TOOLS

- Six 4-inch tartlet pans
- 1-inch lightning bolt–shaped cookie cutter

Remove the frozen piecrusts from the freezer 45 minutes before using. Preheat the oven to 375°F.

Use a rolling pin to roll out the frozen piecrusts, and line the tartlet pans with the dough. Use your fingers to flute the dough around the edge of each tartlet pan. Use a fork to pierce two sets of holes in the piecrust dough. If desired, use the extra dough to create decorations like the ones seen on page 103, using a small lightning bolt cookie cutter and yellow sanding sugar. Create the glasses by cutting out some small circles and shaping the nose piece and arms. Color the glasses by adding some black food coloring to an egg wash and painting on the dough.

In a medium bowl, combine the breadcrumbs, golden syrup, ginger, blackstrap molasses, and lemon. Stir to combine. Pour the mixture into the crusts in the tartlet pans.

Place the tartlets in the oven and bake until they are lightly browned all around, 20 to 25 minutes.

Remove the tartlets when each of them is golden brown and set them aside to cool.

Decorate as desired and serve the treacle tartlets warm with a scoop of whipped cream.

"OCULUS REPARO. THAT'S BETTER, ISN'T IT?"

—Hermione Granger, *Harry Potter and the Sorcerer's Stone*

HOGWARTS CASTLE TRIFLE

YIELD: 16 to 18 servings

Layered with enchantment and flavor, this Hogwarts Castle Trifle is a showstopping dessert inspired by the legendary school of magic. Cream cheese vanilla pound cake is nestled within the trifle, with an additional portion baked in a "Hogwarts in the Snow" cake pan to crown the creation. Miraculous swirls of vanilla bean custard, homemade fresh raspberry syrup, and clouds of Whipped Cream (page 148) create a majestic, edible landscape. The chocolate towers mimic the castle's soaring towers and turrets, whereas the cake and cream evoke the rolling grounds surrounding Hogwarts. Just like the castle, with its 142 staircases, deep dungeons, and magical history dating back to 993, this trifle holds delightful surprises in every bite.

CAKE LAYERS:

- 1½ cups plus 2 tablespoons butter, softened and divided
- 8 ounces cream cheese, softened
- 3 cups granulated sugar
- 1 vanilla bean pod
- 6 large eggs, room temperature
- 3 cups all-purpose flour
- 1 teaspoon baking powder
- 1 pinch sea salt

CUSTARD PUDDING LAYERS:

- 3 tablespoons cornstarch
- 3 cups whole milk, divided
- ¼ teaspoon pink Himalayan sea salt
- 1 cup sugar
- 3 egg yolks
- 1 vanilla bean pod
- 1 tablespoon butter, softened

RASPBERRY SYRUP:

- 1 cup granulated sugar
- 1 cup fresh raspberries
- 1 cup water
- 1 teaspoon cornstarch

ASSEMBLY:

- 2 ounces white chocolate
- 1 recipe Whipped Cream (page 148)
- 2 tablespoons powdered sugar
- 1 teaspoon silver luster dust (optional)

SPECIALTY TOOLS

- Hogwarts in the Snow cake pan set: InsightEditions.com
- Clear glass trifle bowl

To MAKE THE CAKE LAYERS:

Preheat the oven to 350°F. With 2 tablespoons of butter, grease the inside of the Hogwarts cake pan and a 9-by-5-inch loaf pan.

In the bowl of a stand mixer, or in a large bowl with a handheld mixer, cream the remaining 1½ cups of butter and the cream cheese on high speed for 1 to 2 minutes.

Continue beating while slowly adding the sugar. Beat on high speed for 1 to 2 minutes.

Use a paring knife to open the vanilla bean pod and scrape the inside. Discard the pod. Add the vanilla to the mixer and beat for another minute.

Reduce the speed to low and add the eggs, one at a time. Add the flour, baking powder, and sea salt and mix at medium speed just until well combined.

Fill the Hogwarts pan two-thirds full of cake batter. Be careful not to fill the entire cavity to ensure the cake does not bake up over the edge. Pour the remaining cake batter in the loaf pan. Bake the cakes in the oven until a toothpick comes out of the center clean, 75 to 90 minutes.

Remove the cakes and set aside to cool, about 1 hour. When the cakes have cooled for 1 to 2 hours, remove them from the pans.

When the cakes have cooled completely, cut the cake from the loaf pan into ½-inch squares.

To MAKE THE CUSTARD PUDDING LAYERS:

In a large mixing bowl, whisk the cornstarch and ¼ cup of milk.

In a medium saucepan over medium heat, whisk together the remaining 2¾ cups of milk, salt, and sugar. Cook, stirring occasionally, until there is steam, 3 to 5 minutes.

In a medium bowl, whisk the egg yolks. Pour ½ cup of the steamed milk into the egg yolks and stir constantly. Slowly add the egg mixture and the cornstarch mixture into the saucepan and simmer, whisking constantly, until the mixture thickens, 5 to 7 minutes.

Use a paring knife to open the vanilla bean pod and scrape the vanilla from the pod. Discard the pod. Set the vanilla from the pod on a medium plate on the countertop.

Remove the pudding from the heat; stir in the butter and the vanilla that was scraped from the pod. Set aside to cool.

To MAKE THE RASPBERRY SYRUP:

In a medium saucepan over low-medium heat, combine the sugar, raspberries, and water. Stir constantly until the sugar is dissolved. Bring the mixture to a boil. Add the cornstarch. Reduce the heat to low and simmer until thickened, 2 to 3 minutes.

To ASSEMBLE:

While everything is cooling, make the chocolate towers. In a microwave-safe bowl, melt the chocolate in two 30-second bursts, stirring until completely smooth. Allow the chocolate to cool for 1 to 2 minutes and then pour into the tower mold. You will have a bit of chocolate left over; set aside.

Tap the mold gently to remove any air bubbles, transfer to a plate, and refrigerate for about 2 hours or until completely set. Gently remove from the mold. Remelt the leftover chocolate and use it to "glue" each tower onto its spot on the cake.

Place one-third of the square pieces of cake in the bottom of the trifle dish, laying them flat and making sure they are against the sides of the bowl. Add a layer of the pudding, followed by the raspberry syrup, followed by the whipped cream. Repeat these layers until you don't have any more cake, and then top with the Hogwarts cake. Sprinkle with the powdered sugar to create a snowy scene. If using, lightly sprinkle the top with silver luster dust.

"EVERY DAY, EVERY HOUR, THIS VERY MINUTE PERHAPS, DARK FORCES ATTEMPT TO PENETRATE THIS CASTLE'S WALLS. BUT IN THE END, THEIR GREATEST WEAPON . . . IS YOU."

—Professor Albus Dumbledore, *Harry Potter and the Half-Blood Prince*

WINGARDIUM LEVIOSA MERINGUES (FLOATING ISLANDS)

YIELD: 4 servings

Light, airy, and ethereal, these Floating Islands are a tribute to both classic French patisserie and the simple spell that Ron, Hermione, and Harry learn during their first classes at Hogwarts: Wingardium Leviosa!

"It's pronounced leviOsa, not levioSA!" Hermione reminds Ron as they practice their spells.

These levitating scoops of poached meringue "float" in a silky lake of vanilla and bourbon-scented crème anglaise, creating a dessert as delicate as it is indulgent. It's the perfect upscale dessert for a Harry Potter–themed dinner party!

POACHED MERINGUES:

5 egg whites
3½ tablespoons sugar
3 cups milk

CRÈME ANGLAISE:

1½ vanilla beans or ½ teaspoon vanilla extract
½ cup granulated sugar, divided
1 pinch cardamom
6 large egg yolks
2½ teaspoons bourbon (optional)

SPECIALTY TOOLS

Cookie cutter or stencil in the shape of a tall, thin tree

To MAKE THE POACHED MERINGUES:

In the bowl of a stand mixer or a large mixing bowl with a handheld mixer, beat the egg whites and sugar until stiff peaks form, about 6 minutes.

In a large saucepan over high heat, bring the milk to a boil. Reduce the heat to medium. Place two 4-inch oval scoops of meringue in the milk, using a ladle. The meringue will decrease in size when cooking.

Poach the meringues in the milk on one side for about 2 minutes and then flip them gently to the other side and cook until the meringues achieve a firm consistency, about 2 minutes more. Remove the poached meringues and set them on a plate lined with a paper towel to cool. Repeat with remaining meringue. Strain and reserve 2 cups of the poaching milk to make the crème anglaise.

To MAKE THE CRÈME ANGLAISE:

In a saucepan over medium heat, bring the milk used to poach the meringues to a boil and then reduce the heat to medium-low and simmer for about 10 minutes. Break the vanilla beans in half and add them to the milk along with ¼ cup of sugar. Continue to simmer until the mixture thickens, about 10 minutes. Add the cardamom and stir twice to combine.

In the bowl of a stand mixer or a large mixing bowl with a handheld mixer on medium speed, beat the egg yolks until well blended and smooth, about 5 minutes. Gradually add the remaining ¼ cup of sugar while beating. Very slowly pour into the milk mixture. Pour the mixture into the saucepan and return to the stove to continue to simmer over medium heat. Stir constantly until it thickens, about 10 more minutes.

Pull the vanilla beans from the mixture. Add the bourbon (if using) and stir until blended well. Place in the refrigerator until serving.

To ASSEMBLE:

Fill four shallow bowls (soup bowls work well) about three-quarters full with the crème anglaise. Place one large poached meringue into the center of each bowl.

Store the meringues, sauce, and crème anglaise in the refrigerator in separate airtight containers for 1 to 2 days, but they are best eaten immediately.

"ONE OF A WIZARD'S MOST RUDIMENTARY SKILLS IS LEVITATION, OR THE ABILITY TO MAKE OBJECTS FLY."

—Professor Filius Flitwick, *Harry Potter and the Sorcerer's Stone*

CHAPTER 5

DRINKS & FROZEN TREATS

HERBOLOGY BASIL MILKSHAKE

YIELD: 4 small servings or 1 large serving

This creamy vanilla milkshake gets an unexpected twist from homemade fresh basil syrup, topped with vibrant basil sprigs. The refreshing, herbaceous flavor pays tribute to Professor Sprout and her whimsical greenhouse. As Professor of Herbology, Sprout is no stranger to earthy flavors, and this beautifully green treat would surely be a hit after a long day of planting and cultivating magical ingredients, especially after dealing with those Mandrakes.

MILKSHAKE:
- 2 cups packed vanilla ice cream
- ½ cup whole milk
- 4 tablespoons Slytherin Syrup (page 91)
- 1 drop green food coloring (optional)
- 4 basil sprigs, for garnish

To MAKE THE MILKSHAKE:
In a blender, pulse the ice cream, milk, and Slytherin house syrup until well blended. Add the food coloring. Pour the ice cream into fountain glasses. Garnish with the fresh basil.

"DO YOU KNOW THERE'S A WIZARD IN NEPAL WHO'S GROWING GRAVITY-RESISTANT TREES?"

—Neville Longbottom, *Harry Potter and the Goblet of Fire*

HONEY-ROASTED PUMPKIN PATCH SMOOTHIE

YIELD: 4 to 6 servings

This creamy Honey-Roasted Pumpkin Patch Smoothie is a tribute to Hagrid's sprawling pumpkin patch, featured in *Harry Potter and the Prisoner of Azkaban* during the memorable scene where Harry, Ron, and Hermione use a Time-Turner to rescue Buckbeak after he was unfairly sentenced to death. (Take that, Malfoy!) Made with velvety pumpkin purée, rich coconut milk, a drizzle of honey, and a dash of nutmeg, it's a cozy and cold delight topped with a cloud of Whipped Cream (page 148). The earthy sweetness of pumpkin evokes the warmth of autumn at Hogwarts, whereas the comforting flavors are as heartening as Hagrid's care for his magical creatures.

SMOOTHIE:

- 2 cups pumpkin purée
- 2 cups ice cubes
- One 13-ounce can coconut milk
- ⅓ cup honey
- 1 teaspoon plus ¼ teaspoon ground nutmeg, divided
- 1 recipe Whipped Cream (page 148)

In a blender, combine the pumpkin, ice cubes, coconut milk, honey, and 1 teaspoon nutmeg. Pulse three or four times on high until well blended.

Pour into clear glasses. Top with whipped cream and a pinch of the ground nutmeg.

"BUT WHERE IS IT? I SAW THE BEAST, JUST NOW. NOT A MOMENT AGO!"

—Cornelius Fudge,
Harry Potter and the Prisoner of Azkaban

ROMILDA'S ROMANCE FIZZ

YIELD: 4 servings

Bubbly, bright, and blushing red, this sweet concoction is a playful dessert drink that's sure to charm even the sourest dinner guests. Homemade raspberry ice pops are placed in glasses and topped with sparkling wine, creating a fizzy reaction that mirrors the sparks of new romance. The melting ice pop turns the drink a vibrant red, whereas rose petals and herbs like lavender, lemon balm, and spearmint add a fragrant flourish. Inspired by Romilda Vane's attempt to make Ron fall in love with her in *Harry Potter and the Half-Blood Prince*, this drink is sweet without the side effects. For extra flavor, drizzle in your favorite sauce—like the Luna Lovegood Sweet Radish Sauce (page 89)—and toast to love, mischief, and magic.

- 1 cup fresh raspberries
- 1 cup granulated sugar
- 1 cup water
- ½ cup dried rose petals, divided
- 1 large bottle sparkling wine, such as prosecco
- ½ cup chopped fresh romance herbs, such as lavender, lemon balm, or spearmint, divided

SPECIALTY TOOLS

- One 8-by-5-inch silicone ice pop mold with at least 4 cavities
- Sticks for ice pops

"SEE THAT GIRL OVER THERE? THAT'S ROMILDA VANE. APPARENTLY, SHE'S TRYING TO SMUGGLE YOU A LOVE POTION."

—Hermione Granger, *Harry Potter and the Half-Blood Prince*

In a medium saucepan over medium-high heat, combine the raspberries, sugar, and water. Bring to a boil, stirring occasionally. Reduce the heat and simmer until thickened, 2 to 3 minutes.

Remove the sauce from the heat and set aside to cool. When cool, place the sauce in the refrigerator for 15 to 20 minutes or overnight.

When the sauce is completely cooled, add ¼ cup of rose petals and stir to combine. Pour it into four of the cavities in the ice pop mold. Place a stick in the center of each ice pop, ensuring one-third of the stick extends above the ice pop.

Place the mold in the freezer for 6 to 8 hours or overnight. To keep the mold sturdy, place it in an 8-inch square baking dish.

Remove the ice pops from the mold and place each one in a clear glass. Fill each glass two-thirds full with sparkling wine. Sprinkle the remaining rose petals and fresh romance herbs in and around the love potions.

COLOR-CHANGING BREW

YIELD: 4 servings

Bold and mesmerizing, this Color-Changing Brew is a drink worthy of Severus Snape's Potions classroom. Inspired by his thick golden potion used to treat Dumbledore's cursed hand, this drink is equally dramatic—minus the Dark magic. Butterfly pea flower tea gives the drink a striking blue hue, but with a drop of fresh lemon juice, it transforms into a deep, enchanting purple. Made with lemon-lime soda, fresh mint, and loose-leaf butterfly pea flower tea, it's refreshing with a twist of alchemy. This recipe includes instructions for each guest to brew their own tea, creating a delightful, color-changing potion experience right at the table. No wand needed—just a dash of curiosity.

- 4 teaspoons butterfly pea flower loose tea (or 4 bags)
- 2 cups water
- 4 cups lemon-lime soda
- 2 cups ice
- 4 fresh lemons
- 4 large mint sprigs

SPECIALTY TOOLS

- 4 loose-leaf tea diffuser baskets (optional)

Place the tea in a clear glass teacup or a glass with a pedestal or stem. Add ½ cup of hot water to each glass. Let the tea steep for a few minutes.

Add ½ cup of lemon-lime soda to each glass.

Divide the ice evenly among the glasses.

Cut the lemons in half and slice a thin piece off each lemon as a garnish for each potion. Place a fresh sprig of mint on the rim of each glass with the lemon slice garnish.

Squeeze the desired amount of lemon juice into the glass and stir.

"SHOULD YOU EVER STEAL FROM MY PERSONAL STORES AGAIN, MY HAND MIGHT JUST SLIP OVER YOUR MORNING PUMPKIN JUICE."

—Professor Severus Snape,
Harry Potter and the Goblet of Fire

PREFECT BATHROOM BUBBLES

YIELD: 4 servings

In *Harry Potter and the Goblet of Fire*, Harry famously takes a bath with his golden dragon's egg in the prefects' bathroom. "You know the prefects' bathroom on the fifth floor?" Cedric Diggory asks Harry. "It's not a bad place for a bath."

This frothy, bubbly egg cream takes a nod from Harry's bubble bath with his dragon's egg, but don't worry—no dragon eggs were harmed in the making of this delicious treat! Though classic egg creams are made with chocolate syrup, this variation swaps in a rich, homemade toffee syrup for a buttery, caramellike flavor. The drink is a simple combination of club soda, milk, and syrup. Garnish with a sprinkle of gold sugar crystals and stars for a touch of elegance.

EGG CREAM:

- 6 cups club soda
- 3 cups whole milk
- ½ cup toffee syrup (use store-bought or see the recipe here)
- 2 cups ice cubes
- 1 teaspoon gold sugar crystals and stars, for garnish

TOFFEE SYRUP:

- 1 cup light brown sugar
- ½ cup heavy (whipping) cream
- 1 teaspoon vanilla extract
- ½ cup butter, softened
- ½ teaspoon coarse salt

SPECIALTY TOOLS

- 4 milkshake glasses
- 4 long ice-cream spoons (optional)

TO MAKE THE EGG CREAM:

Divide the soda, milk, and syrup evenly in the glasses and stir vigorously to combine well. Divide the ice among the glasses. Sprinkle the top of each glass with ¼ teaspoon of gold sugar crystals and stars. Serve with a straw and ice-cream spoon, if desired.

TO MAKE THE TOFFEE SYRUP:

In a large saucepan over medium heat, combine the brown sugar, heavy cream, vanilla, butter, and salt. When the sugar is dissolved, bring the mixture to a boil, stirring constantly. Reduce the heat and simmer for 2 to 3 minutes. Remove from heat and set aside to cool, 15 to 20 minutes.

This recipe will make more than is needed for four egg cream drinks. The rest of the syrup can be stored in an airtight container in the refrigerator for 4 to 5 days.

HOUSE SODAS

YIELD: 4 servings of each soda

SLYTHERIN SODA POP

Slytherin Soda Pop is a sweet, invigorating drink made with fresh green basil, simple syrup, and sparkling water. Just like the Slytherin common room beneath the Black Lake, this soda is mysterious and enchanting, with a lively green hue reminiscent of the house's emblematic emerald color. Whether you're channeling ambition or simply enjoying a fizzy treat, this soda is a delicious way to embrace the Slytherin spirit.

- 4 cups sparkling water
- 2 cups ice
- 4 tablespoons Slytherin Syrup (page 91)
- 4 basil sprigs, for garnish

SPECIALTY TOOLS
4 cocktail skewers

Divide the sparkling water and ice among four glasses, followed by the syrup. Stir well with a spoon. Garnish with fresh basil on a cocktail skewer.

RAVENCLAW SODA POP

This deeply hued drink boasts a natural blue color from butterfly pea flowers, representing Ravenclaw's iconic blue and silver. Just as Ravenclaw students are known for their sharp minds and curiosity, this soda offers a clever blend of sweet and spicy flavors. Whether you're enjoying it while studying or celebrating a creative achievement, Ravenclaw Soda Pop is the perfect drink for those who value knowledge and imagination. For an extra touch of vibrancy, add a few drops of blue food coloring!

- 4 cups sparkling water
- 2 cups ice
- 4 tablespoons Ravenclaw Syrup (page 91)
- 8 small pieces candied ginger, for garnish

SPECIALTY TOOLS
4 cocktail skewers

Divide the sparkling water and ice among four glasses, followed by the syrup. Stir well with a spoon. Garnish with two pieces of candied ginger on a cocktail skewer.

GRYFFINDOR SODA POP

Gryffindor Soda Pop, made with fresh raspberries and raspberry simple syrup, showcases the house's scarlet color. Just as Gryffindor house is known for its courage and determination, this soda delivers a vibrant burst of flavor that packs a punch. Representing the element of fire, the drink mirrors the fiery spirit of Gryffindor students, who must pass the Fat Lady's portrait to enter their common room in the highest tower of Hogwarts. Whether you're embracing a daring adventure or enjoying a sweet, fizzy treat, Gryffindor Soda Pop is the perfect drink for those brave at heart.

- 4 cups sparkling water
- 2 cups ice
- 4 tablespoons Gryffindor Syrup (page 91)
- 8 fresh whole raspberries, for garnish

SPECIALTY TOOLS

4 cocktail skewers

Divide the sparkling water and ice among four glasses, followed by the syrup. Stir well with a spoon. Garnish with two whole raspberries on a cocktail skewer.

HUFFLEPUFF SODA POP

This lemony yellow soda is an ode to the spirit of Hufflepuff, known for its values of dedication, patience, and loyalty. Made with citrusy lemon syrup, Hufflepuff Soda Pop mirrors the house color of yellow, offering a bright and zingy flavor. Just as Hufflepuff students are dedicated and grounded, this drink is simple yet uplifting. The lemon color honors Cedric Diggory's legacy as a true Hufflepuff hero. Whether you're celebrating loyalty or simply enjoying a moment of refreshment, this soda is a tribute to the hardworking and fair-minded members of Hufflepuff.

- 4 cups sparkling water
- 2 cups ice
- 4 tablespoons Hufflepuff Syrup (page 91)
- 4 lemon slices, for garnish

SPECIALTY TOOLS

4 cocktail skewers

Divide the sparkling water and ice among four glasses, followed by the syrup. Stir well with a spoon. Garnish with one lemon slice on a cocktail skewer.

BRANDY AFFOGATO

YIELD: 1 serving

This Brandy Affogato is inspired by the iconic moment when Dumbledore asks Hagrid for a cup of tea or a large brandy after Buckbeak is saved from a most terrible fate. Rich homemade ricotta gelato forms the creamy base, though any favorite flavor will do. A generous pour of any brandy—one of the finest for desserts—adds deep, syrupy notes that melt into the gelato, creating a luscious, boozy treat. The brandy's warmth contrasts beautifully with the cold gelato, offering a layered dessert fit for a cozy night in.

GELATO:

4 egg yolks

1 tablespoon granulated sugar

1 cup heavy (whipping) cream

½ cup whole milk

½ cup honey

¼ teaspoon sea salt

1 cup strained ricotta cheese

TOPPING:

2 tablespoons ground espresso beans (4 tablespoons for a double shot)

4 tablespoons water

1 tablespoon brandy

3 to 5 golden raisins

SPECIALTY TOOLS

Espresso maker

Ice-cream maker

To MAKE THE GELATO:

In a medium mixing bowl, use a wire whisk to combine the egg yolks and sugar, forming a paste.

In a medium saucepan over low-medium heat, combine the heavy cream, milk, honey, and sea salt. Simmer until the mixture starts to bubble, 5 to 6 minutes.

Slowly combine the egg mixture with the milk mixture, adding in a little at a time, stirring constantly.

Reduce the heat to low and gently stir the mixture until it thickens, 5 to 6 minutes.

Strain the mixture through a fine-mesh strainer. Add the ricotta cheese to the mixture and stir well to combine thoroughly.

Place the mixture in the refrigerator for 2 to 3 hours or overnight. Follow the ice-cream maker's instructions on how to process the mixture.

This recipe will make more gelato than is needed for one affogato. Store the remaining gelato in the freezer in an airtight container for 1 to 2 weeks.

To MAKE THE TOPPING:

Place the ground espresso beans in the filter of the espresso machine. Tamp (press down on) the espresso grounds. Add the water and process the mixture through the machine according to the machine's instructions.

Place a few small scoops of the gelato in a clear, stemmed glass. Top with the espresso and brandy. Garnish with the golden raisins.

"MEANWHILE, I'D LIKE A NICE CUP OF TEA OR A LARGE BRANDY. OH, EXECUTIONER, YOUR SERVICES ARE NO LONGER REQUIRED. THANK YOU."

—Professor Albus Dumbledore, *Harry Potter and the Prisoner of Azkaban*

DIVINATION TEA COCKTAIL

YIELD: 4 servings

This mystical brew is inspired by Professor Trelawney's dramatic tea leaf reading in *Harry Potter and the Prisoner of Azkaban*, where she ominously declared, "Oh my dear boy. My dear. You have the Grim!"

This cocktail captures the essence of that fateful moment with linden tea, a splash of dark berry juice, and a bubbly finish of prosecco or sparkling wine. A nod to Trelawney's own prophecy about Voldemort and the Chosen One, this enchanting drink is perfect for raising a glass to fate, foresight, and the unknown.

4 teaspoons loose-leaf linden tea (it must be loose to read the tea)
2 cups water
2 cups ice
1 bottle sparkling wine, like prosecco or champagne, chilled
4 tablespoons berry juice or fruit punch
8 berries, for garnish
4 sprigs fresh mint, for garnish
4 thin slices fresh lemon peel, for garnish

SPECIALTY TOOLS

4 heat-safe cups
4 champagne flutes or wineglasses
4 bamboo cocktail skewers, for garnish

Place 1 teaspoon of tea in each of the four heat-safe cups. Add ½ cup of hot water in each and steep for 2 to 3 minutes.

Divide the ice among the four champagne flutes or wineglasses. Fill each glass half full of the sparkling wine. Divide the berry juice among the glasses.

When the tea has cooled to room temperature, add ½ cup of tea to each glass.

Place the berries, mint, and lemon peel on the four skewers and garnish each glass with a skewer.

"BROADEN YOUR MINDS. YOUR AURA IS PULSING, DEAR. ARE YOU IN THE BEYOND?"

—Professor Sybill Trelawney,
Harry Potter and the Prisoner of Azkaban

KNICKERBOCKER GLORY

YIELD: 4 sundaes

Celebrate the spirited rivalry of Hogwarts houses with this dazzling Knickerbocker Glory sundae, a towering, layered ice-cream treat popular in the UK. Just as house points at Hogwarts reflected the achievements and competitions between Gryffindor, Hufflepuff, Ravenclaw, and Slytherin, this sundae features bold homemade syrups representing each house. Scoops of creamy vanilla ice cream are topped with bold red raspberry (Gryffindor), zesty yellow lemon (Hufflepuff), refreshing green basil (Slytherin), and sweet blue ginger (Ravenclaw) syrups. Finished with a cloud of Whipped Cream (page 148), sparkling gold sugar crystals, stars, and a cherry on top, this sundae is as showstopping as a Quidditch victory.

Slytherin: Green (basil)
Ravenclaw: Blue (ginger)
Gryffindor: Red (raspberry)
Hufflepuff: Yellow (lemon)

SUNDAE:

6 cups vanilla ice cream
House Syrups (page 90)
1 recipe Whipped Cream (page 148)
1 teaspoon gold sugar crystals and stars, for topping
4 maraschino cherries, stems on
4 Lightning Bolt Candy Mints (page 27), for garnish (optional)

SPECIALTY TOOLS

4 milkshake glasses
Sundae spoons

To ASSEMBLE THE SUNDAE:

Divide the ice cream among the four glasses. Use a spoon to drizzle 1 to 2 tablespoons of the four syrups into each glass. Top with more ice cream and whipped cream. Garnish with the gold sugar crystals and stars and top with a maraschino cherry. Garnish with other sweets, like one of the candy mints.

"AT THE END OF THE YEAR, THE HOUSE WITH THE MOST POINTS IS AWARDED THE HOUSE CUP."

—Professor Minerva McGonagall, *Harry Potter and the Sorcerer's Stone*

CHAPTER 6

BUTTERBEER-INSPIRED TREATS

BUTTERBEER-INSPIRED CANDY

YIELD: 48 bite-size pieces

The flavor of these hard candies is inspired by the beloved wizarding world drink favored by Harry, Ron, and Hermione. Butterbeer is first introduced to the friend group in *Harry Potter and the Prisoner of Azkaban* and remains a sought-after treat throughout the series. Luckily, you don't need to visit the Leaky Cauldron to enjoy the taste of Butterbeer as long as you have this recipe, though there's nothing quite like a real Butterbeer. These candies are smooth and creamy and can be taken on the go for a bit of Butterbeer-inspired flavor any time you want!

- 1½ cups granulated sugar
- ¾ cup water
- ⅔ cup corn syrup
- ½ teaspoon cream of tartar
- ½ teaspoon butterscotch extract
- 8 to 10 drops yellow food coloring

SPECIALTY TOOLS

- Candy thermometer
- Candy mold (optional)

Line two 13-by-18-inch baking sheets with parchment paper.

In a large saucepan over medium heat, combine the sugar, water, corn syrup, cream of tartar, and butterscotch extract. Bring the mixture to a boil, then continue to cook until the temperature reaches 300°F on a candy thermometer.

Remove the candy from the heat and add the food coloring. Stir well to combine, ensuring there are no streaks of color in the candy.

Quickly spread the mixture on the baking sheets or place the mixture into candy molds.

Let the mixture rest until hardened, 1 to 2 hours.

When the candy has hardened, break it up into bite-size pieces or, if using candy molds, remove the candy from the candy molds.

"DOES ANYONE FANCY A BUTTERBEER?"

—Harry Potter, *Harry Potter and the Half-Blood Prince*

THE THREE BROOMSTICKS WHITE CHOCOLATE BARK

YIELD: 50 servings, depending on the size of the pieces

Rich and silky and inspired by the warm flavor of Butterbeer, this white chocolate bark is a treat worthy of any wizarding celebration. Made with melted white chocolate and crushed butterscotch hard candies, it's a fine tribute to the beloved drink. Butterbeer was a favorite among Hogwarts students, served both hot and cold at the Three Broomsticks—where Harry, Ron, and Hermione enjoyed it in *Harry Potter and the Half-Blood Prince*. Its buttery notes and hint of sweetness made it a comforting choice, much like this bark. Perfect for sharing, it's a delicious nod to one of the wizarding world's most iconic flavors.

1 teaspoon coconut oil

One 11-ounce bag white chocolate chips

One 10-ounce bag butterscotch hard candies

4 tablespoons gold sugar crystals and stars

In a double boiler over medium-low heat, or in a microwave-safe bowl in the microwave, combine the coconut oil and the chocolate. Heat until the chocolate melts. If using the microwave, microwave for 1 minute, stirring after 30 seconds, until it is well melted and combined and there are no lumps.

Put the butterscotch candies in a food processor and pulse them two or three times until they are crushed. A few larger pieces might remain. These can provide texture.

Add all the crushed candy, except 2 tablespoons, to the melted chocolate. Use a spoon to stir to blend the crushed candy in with the chocolate well.

Spread the mixture to about ¼ inch thick on a 13-by-18-inch baking sheet lined with parchment paper. Ensure the thickness is the same throughout. Sprinkle the remaining 2 tablespoons of crushed candy evenly over the mixture, then sprinkle the sugar crystals and stars.

Let the mixture dry and set, about 2 hours.

When the mixture is dry and set, use your hands to break it up into 2-inch pieces. The pieces will be different sizes and shapes and have jagged edges.

Arrange these pieces of candy on a dish to serve guests, or wrap a few pieces in clear cellophane bags to give guests as gifts to take home.

"THE THREE BROOMSTICKS AND I GO WAY BACK, FURTHER THAN I'D LIKE TO ADMIT. I CAN REMEMBER WHEN IT WAS ONE BROOMSTICK!"

—Professor Horace Slughorn,
Harry Potter and the Half-Blood Prince

OTTER PATRONUS BUTTERSCOTCH BISCUITS

YIELD: 12 cookies

Hermione's Patronus, an otter, symbolizes her intelligence, loyalty, and playful spirit. These charming biscuits pay tribute to her otter Patronus with an enchanting combination of brown sugar, butterscotch, and hearty oats, reminiscent of classic English oat biscuits. Cut into otter shapes and dipped in smooth chocolate, these cookies have a crisp, buttery texture with a creamy kick from the butterscotch extract. The icing details, such as eyes, mouth, and delicate whiskers, will help bring the otters to life. Enjoy these biscuits with a cup of tea or when you are craving a Butterbeer.

DOUGH:

½ cup (1 stick) butter

1 cup dark brown sugar

2 tablespoons golden syrup, corn syrup, or maple syrup

1 teaspoon butterscotch extract

⅔ cup rolled oats

1 cup whole wheat flour, plus more as needed

½ teaspoon baking powder

½ teaspoon baking soda

¼ teaspoon pink Himalayan sea salt

CHOCOLATE TOPPING:

16 ounces semisweet chocolate

1 tablespoon coconut oil or olive oil

Black food coloring

SPECIALTY TOOLS

Cookie cutter in the shape of an otter, 3.18 by 3.7 inches

"JUST REMEMBER, YOUR PATRONUS CAN ONLY PROTECT YOU FOR AS LONG AS YOU STAY FOCUSED."

—Harry Potter, *Harry Potter and the Order of the Phoenix*

TO MAKE THE COOKIES:

Preheat the oven to 350°F.

In the bowl of a stand mixer, or in a large bowl with a handheld mixer, cream the butter and sugar on high speed until fluffy, 1 to 2 minutes. Add the golden syrup and butterscotch extract to the bowl and continue to mix to combine. Reduce the speed to medium and add the oats, flour, baking powder, baking soda, and sea salt.

Roll the dough into a ball, cover it with plastic wrap or parchment paper, and refrigerate for 20 to 30 minutes.

Use a rolling pin to roll out the dough ¼ inch thick. Add more flour as needed to keep the dough from sticking.

Use the cookie cutter to cut out the otter shapes. Place the cookies on a 13-by-18-inch baking sheet lined with parchment paper.

Bake the cookies in the oven until they are just slightly browned, 10 to 12 minutes.

Remove the cookies from the oven and set them aside to cool.

TO MAKE THE DIPPING CHOCOLATE:

In a microwave oven or a double boiler on the stovetop, combine the chocolate and coconut oil and slowly stir while heating. Stir until well melted and combined and there are no lumps in the chocolate.

When the cookies are cool, dip the bottom (flat side) of each cookie in the melted chocolate. Set the cookies aside for the chocolate to harden, about 10 minutes. Add the black food coloring to the remaining chocolate.

Once the base chocolate is set, pipe the chocolate to create the eyes, nose, whiskers, and any other decoration you'd like.

BUTTERSCOTCH CHIP COOKIES

YIELD: 40 cookies

Warm chocolate chip cookies may be the ultimate comfort treat, but just wait until you try their buttery, gooey counterpart: Butterscotch Chip Cookies. There's nothing more soothing than a warm Butterbeer on a winter day in Hogsmeade, except maybe one of these cookies. This soft, chewy cookie is a fun take on a classic recipe. We think Harry, Ron, and Hermione would have gladly taken a bite if offered during one of their field trips from Hogwarts. If you want to cut the sweetness just a bit, feel free to omit the marshmallows.

- ¾ cup light brown sugar
- ¾ cup granulated sugar
- 1 cup (2 sticks) butter, softened
- 2 large eggs
- 2 teaspoons butterscotch extract
- 2½ cups all-purpose flour
- 1 teaspoon baking soda
- 1 teaspoon sea salt
- 2 cups butterscotch morsels
- 3 cups mini marshmallows
- ½ cup Butterbeer-Inspired Sauce (page 140)

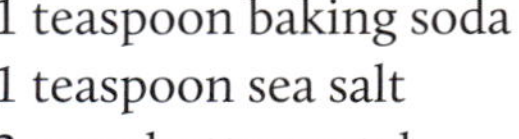

"NOW REMEMBER, THESE VISITS TO HOGSMEADE VILLAGE ARE A PRIVILEGE. SHOULD YOUR BEHAVIOR REFLECT POORLY ON THE SCHOOL IN ANY WAY, THAT PRIVILEGE SHALL NOT BE EXTENDED AGAIN."

—Professor Minerva McGonagall,
Harry Potter and the Prisoner of Azkaban

Preheat the oven to 375°F.

In the bowl of a stand mixer, or in a large mixing bowl using a handheld mixer on medium speed, cream together the sugars and butter.

Add the eggs, one at a time. Add the butterscotch extract.

Add the flour, baking soda, and sea salt, mixing well to combine all the ingredients together.

Stir the butterscotch morsels into the dough, making sure the morsels are evenly distributed.

Form the dough into 1-inch round balls and place them on a parchment paper–lined 9-by-13-inch baking sheet. Arrange the balls of dough in rows. Place the balls 2 inches apart. Lightly press down on each ball of dough.

Bake the cookies in the oven until they are golden brown and lift up around the edges, 10 to 12 minutes.

Remove the cookies from the oven and set them aside to cool. Quickly press five or six mini marshmallows onto the top of each of the cookies when the cookies are still warm so they stick.

When the cookies have cooled, use a spoon to drizzle Butterbeer-Inspired Sauce on each of the cookies.

VANILLA BUTTERSCOTCH CAKE

YIELD: 16 servings (this is a double batch for 3 cake pans)

Though Butterbeer traditionally comes in liquid form, every bite of this cake will remind you of sipping a tall mug of Butterbeer in Hogsmeade. This cake could easily be served alongside some of Molly Weasley's most delicious sweets on Christmas Day or on the Hogwarts' table during an elaborate feast. With heaps of marshmallows and Butterbeer-Inspired Sauce (page 140), this cake is as adorable as it is tasty.

- 2 cups (4 sticks) plus 2 tablespoons butter, softened and divided
- 2 cups granulated sugar, divided
- 8 large eggs, room temperature
- 3⅓ cups cake flour
- 4 teaspoons baking powder
- 2 teaspoons sea salt
- 4 tablespoons butterscotch extract
- 1 cup whole milk
- 1 tablespoon gold or yellow-colored sparkle sugar
- 2 cups jumbo marshmallows
- 2 cups mini marshmallows
- Butterbeer-Inspired Sauce (page 140)
- Butterbeer-Inspired Candy (page 131)

BUTTERCREAM FROSTING:

- 6 cups powdered sugar
- 1 cup plus 1 tablespoon butter, softened and divided
- 2 teaspoons vanilla
- ¼ cup milk
- 3 or 4 drops yellow food coloring

SPECIALTY TOOLS

- Three 9-inch round cake pans

"ON CHRISTMAS EVE NIGHT, WE AND OUR GUESTS GATHER IN THE GREAT HALL FOR A NIGHT OF WELL-MANNERED FRIVOLITY."

—Professor Minerva McGonagall, *Harry Potter and the Goblet of Fire*

To MAKE THE CAKE:

Preheat the oven to 350°F.

Use 2 tablespoons of butter to generously grease the inside of three 9-inch round cake pans.

In the bowl of a stand mixer, or in a large bowl with a handheld mixer, cream the remaining 2 cups of butter and the sugar on medium-high until smooth, 1 to 2 minutes.

Add the eggs, one at a time, beating on medium speed constantly. Add half of the flour, the baking powder, and sea salt and stir until well combined. Add the butterscotch extract and half the milk and stir until well combined. Repeat until all the cake ingredients are well combined.

Pour the cake batter in the cake pans and put them in the oven. Bake the cakes until they are golden brown and a toothpick comes out of the center clean, 50 to 60 minutes.

Remove the cakes from the oven and set them on a cooling rack to cool. When the cakes have cooled, remove them from the cake pans.

To MAKE THE BUTTERCREAM FROSTING:

In a large mixing bowl, use a hand mixer to combine the powdered sugar, 1 cup of butter, the vanilla, and milk. Beat on high speed until thickened but still soft enough to decorate the cake. Add the yellow food coloring and mix until smooth and no streaks of color remain.

To ASSEMBLE:

Layer the cakes, placing a layer of frosting between each cake layer.

Use an offset spatula to spread the frosting around the sides of the cake.

Artfully arrange the marshmallows on top of the cake.

Drizzle the Butterbeer-Inspired Sauce over the top of the cake, allowing the sauce to drip down the sides. Break the Butterbeer-Inspired Candy into small pieces and arrange them over the marshmallow mounds.

BUTTERBEER-INSPIRED SAUCE

YIELD: 16 servings

Next time you bite into a delicious dessert and think, *This would be great with some Butterbeer*, simply drizzle on some Butterbeer-Inspired Sauce! Made with the familiar warming flavors of Butterbeer, this sauce is a versatile topping that can be used to top ice creams, dip fruit, or drizzle on cakes and cookies. Sticky and sweet, it's the perfect way to bring a little Butterbeer-esque flavor to every dessert you make!

1 stick (8 tablespoons) butter

¼ cup water

2 tablespoons golden syrup or light corn syrup

1 cup light brown sugar

½ cup heavy (whipping) cream

2 teaspoons vanilla extract

Pinch sea salt

In a heavy-bottomed saucepan, combine the butter, water, and corn syrup and cook over medium-low heat until the butter is melted. Add the brown sugar, raise the heat to medium, and cook until the sugar is dissolved, about 5 minutes. Continue to cook, raising the heat again to medium-high until the mixture begins to boil. Boil for 4 to 8 minutes or until it starts to brown around the edges, stirring the mixture and cooking until it is a dark amber hue.

Remove the pan from the heat and stand back to avoid the spatter. Slowly add the cream, stirring constantly. Once the mixture is smooth, add the vanilla and sea salt. Serve immediately or let cool and store in an airtight container in the refrigerator for up to 2 weeks.

Daily

FROZEN BUTTERSCOTCH

YIELD: 4 servings

Cool, creamy, and irresistibly sweet, this Frozen Butterscotch is a refreshing twist on the beloved wizarding drink. Made with vanilla ice cream blended with homemade butterscotch sauce and milk, then topped with Whipped Cream (page 148), more butterscotch sauce, and gold sugar crystals, it's perfect for festive gatherings. Butterbeer has long been a staple at magical celebrations, from the Yule Ball to the Quidditch World Cup, and even at Bill and Fleur's enchanting wedding (before it was interrupted by the Death Eaters' arrival). Its comforting, indulgent flavor brings warmth to winter feasts and a frosty delight to summer parties. This frozen version captures that same celebratory spirit, offering a chilled, creamy treat that's perfect for toasting to friendship, love, and a little bit of magic.

- 8 cups vanilla ice cream
- ½ cup whole milk
- ½ cup Butterbeer-Inspired Sauce, divided (page 140)
- 2 cups Whipped Cream (page 148)
- 1 tablespoon gold sugar crystals, gold nonpareils, and stars, mixed

In a stand blender or using an immersion blender, combine the ice cream, milk, and ⅓ cup of Butterbeer-Inspired Sauce. Pulse three or four times until well combined. Divide the frozen Butterbeer among four glasses. Top each glass with whipped cream and drizzle with the remaining Butterbeer-Inspired Sauce. Sprinkle the gold sugar crystals and stars on top of the cream.

"STOP IT, RON. YOU'RE MAKING IT SNOW."

—Hermione Granger,
Harry Potter and the Half-Blood Prince

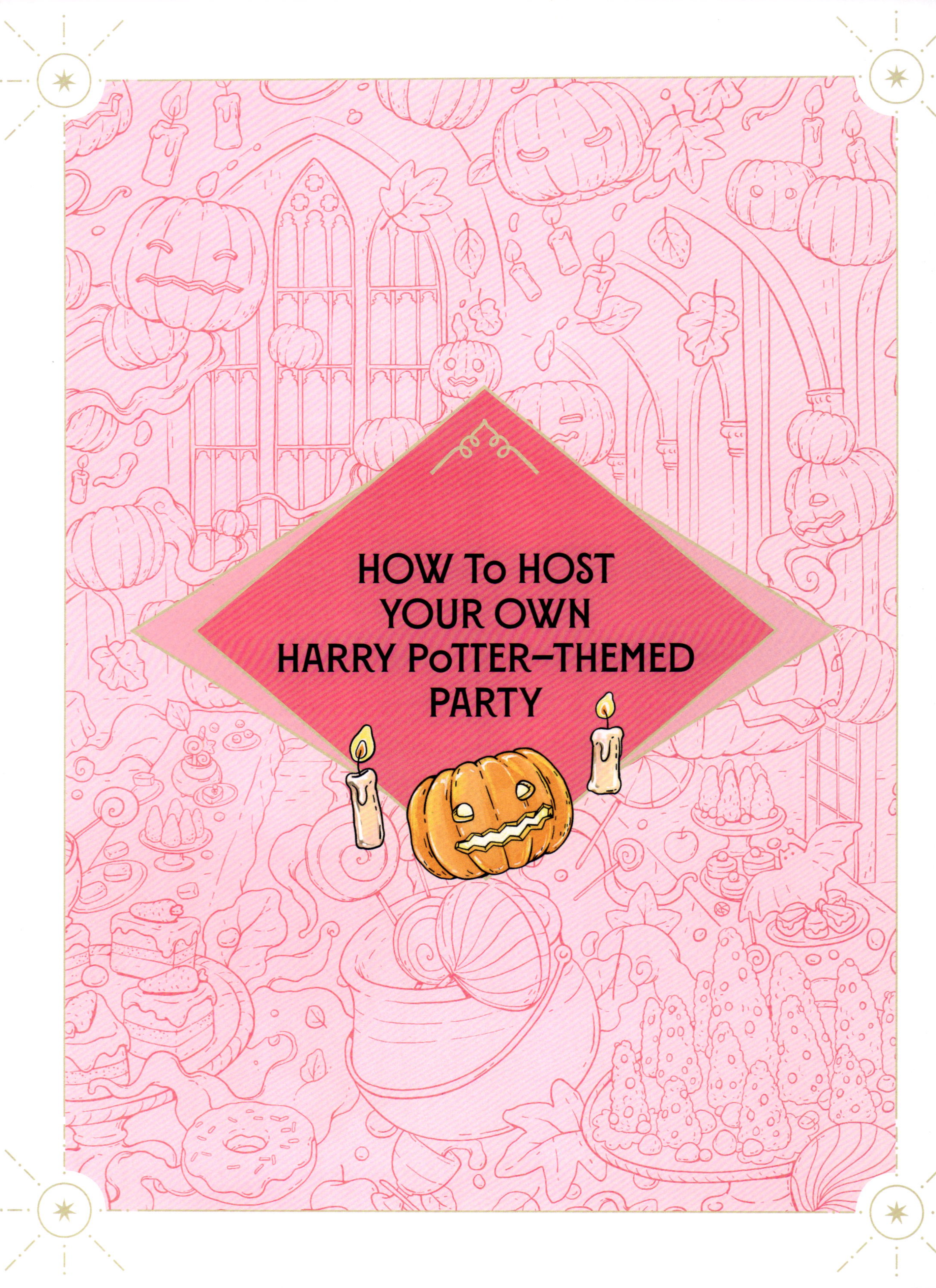

HOW To HOST YOUR OWN HARRY PoTTER–THEMED PARTY

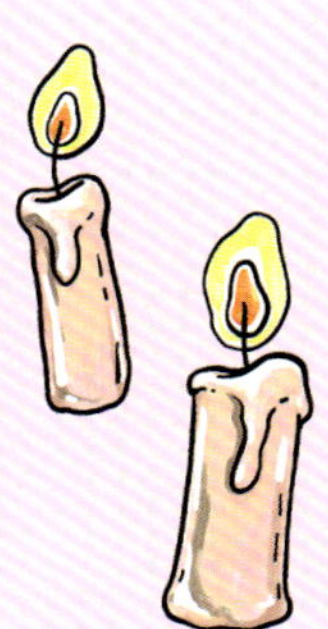

Make the most of your wizarding world gathering with these inexpensive entertaining ideas that capture the mystique of Harry Potter's magical world.

Choose a theme based on a food scene from one of the Harry Potter movies and plan a menu according to the theme. For the scenes that don't show all the food items, have fun imagining foods that might have been served.

PARTY THEME IDEAS

Professor Slughorn's dinner party, *Harry Potter and the Half-Blood Prince*

Molly Weasley's meatball dinner, *Harry Potter and the Order of the Phoenix*

Lunch for Mrs. Mason, *Harry Potter and the Chamber of Secrets*

Dinner for Aunt Marge, *Harry Potter and the Prisoner of Azkaban*

Harry's breakfast on Dudley Dursley's birthday, *Harry Potter and the Sorcerer's Stone*

Drinking Butterbeer at the Three Broomsticks, *Harry Potter and the Half-Blood Prince*

A trip to Honeydukes sweetshop, *Harry Potter and the Prisoner of Azkaban*

A Hogwarts Great Hall feast

The Yule Ball, *Harry Potter and the Goblet of Fire*

DECORATION AND ACTIVITY IDEAS

- Brew a Divination Tea Cocktail (page 125) and have fun imagining what the tea leaves left in your cup might say about you and your future.
- Decorate foods and food displays with inexpensive stencils that resemble Harry Potter–themed images, symbols, and designs. Use cardamom, cocoa powder, or powdered sugar to stencil on cakes, breads, cookies, and more.
- Use miniature cookie cutters to create tiny spooky cutouts in piecrusts to place on cakes, pies, and more.
- Encourage guests to mix and mingle with ice-breaking activities like the name game. Write the names of characters from Harry Potter movies on index cards and tape a card with a name on the back of each guest. Ask them to try to guess who they are by asking other guests only "yes" or "no" questions about the person.
- Play Harry Potter movies on TV screens throughout the house, with the sound turned down, to reinforce the theme.
- In true Hogwarts correspondence style, be sure to personally deliver invitations to guests. Seal the envelopes with wax stamps like Hogwarts acceptance letters. Include a QR code that links to an electronic party-planning application where they can RSVP so you can track who is coming and email reminders.
- Have plenty of fresh and dried herbs throughout the house. Arrange rosemary, sage, and thyme in centerpieces, dessert tables, and candle arrangements. Provide manicure scissors for guests to pick out and cut their own herbs for garnishes.
- Invest in a few Harry Potter–themed accent dishes rather than a whole set of dishes. Serve on platters in the colors of Harry's scarf, the houses of Hogwarts, or the deep purple and black colors that are prominent in the movies.
- Make a centerpiece cake for the middle of the dining table or dessert table, using one of the thematic recipes in this book, like the Flurry of Letters Cake (page 76).
- Host a costume contest with prizes for the costumes that most closely resemble characters from the Harry Potter movies.
- Create a period photo booth and take photos of guests to send after the gathering, with thank-you notes.
- Make your own mini broomsticks with fresh herbs.
- Play a game of Harry Potter movie trivia.

BASICS

The following are basic recipes that are used multiple times throughout this cookbook. When you see a note in the ingredients list such as "Whipped Cream (page 148)," flip back to this page to find what you need!

WHIPPED CREAM

YIELD: 2 cups

This Whipped Cream is the perfect addition to any dessert with its creamy, light, and fluffy texture. Bonus points that it can be whipped up in just a matter of moments.

2 cups heavy (whipping) cream
½ cup granulated sugar
½ teaspoon fresh lemon juice

In a stand mixer or a large mixing bowl with a hand mixer, beat the whipping cream, sugar, and lemon juice together on low until well combined and starting to thicken so it won't splatter, 2 to 3 minutes. Increase the speed to high and beat until thickened enough to form soft peaks, 3 to 4 minutes.

PIECRUST

YIELD: 1 piecrust

This crispy and buttery Piecrust is a superb foundation for an enchanting dessert.

2½ cups all-purpose flour
2 teaspoons powdered sugar
1 teaspoon kosher salt
½ cup unsalted butter, very cold
¼ cup solid vegetable shortening, very cold
½ cup ice water

Preheat the oven to 425°F. In a large bowl, combine the flour, sugar, and salt. Cut the cold butter and shortening into small pieces. Using a pastry cutter or two forks, work the butter into the flour mixture until all the pieces are pea-size or smaller.

Add the ice water a little bit at a time and use the pastry cutter to bring the dough together. As the dough starts to come together, switch to using your hands or a spatula, using up to ½ cup of water, until the dough just comes together.

Split the dough in half, turn out onto a floured surface, and roll out into a round that extends past your 9-inch pie dish. Trim the edge of the dough so that it extends only about ¼ inch past the edge of the pie dish and crimp with your fingers to make a ruffled edge. Prick all over the bottom with a fork and bake for 12 to 15 minutes.

BUTTERCREAM FROSTING

YIELD: 4 cups

This traditional Buttercream Frosting is simple to whip up and is a great addition to any cake.

6 cups powdered sugar
1 cup plus butter, softened
2 teaspoons vanilla extract
¼ cup milk

In a large mixing bowl, use a hand mixer to combine the powdered sugar, butter, vanilla, and milk. Beat on high speed until thickened but still soft enough to decorate.

MEASUREMENT CONVERSIONS

KITCHEN MEASUREMENTS

CUPS	TABLESPOONS	TEASPOONS	FLUID OUNCES
1⁄16 cup	1 tbsp	3 tsp	½ fl oz
⅛ cup	2 tbsp	6 tsp	1 fl oz
¼ cup	4 tbsp	12 tsp	2 fl oz
⅓ cup	5½ tbsp	16 tsp	2⅔ fl oz
½ cup	8 tbsp	24 tsp	4 fl oz
⅔ cup	10⅔ tbsp	32 tsp	5⅓ fl oz
¾ cup	12 tbsp	36 tsp	6 fl oz
1 cup	16 tbsp	48 tsp	8 fl oz

GALLONS	QUARTS	PINTS	CUPS	FLUID OUNCES
1⁄16 gal	¼ qt	½ pt	1 cup	8 fl oz
⅛ gal	½ qt	1 pt	2 cups	16 fl oz
¼ gal	1 qt	2 pt	4 cups	32 fl oz
½ gal	2 qt	4 pt	8 cups	64 fl oz
1 gal	4 qt	8 pt	16 cups	128 fl oz

WEIGHT

GRAMS	OUNCES
14 g	½ oz
28 g	1 oz
57 g	2 oz
85 g	3 oz
113 g	4 oz
142 g	5 oz
170 g	6 oz
283 g	10 oz
397 g	14 oz
454 g	16 oz
907 g	32 oz

OVEN TEMPERATURES

FAHRENHEIT	CELSIUS
200°F	93°C
225°F	107°C
250°F	121°C
275°F	135°C
300°F	149°C
325°F	163°C
350°F	177°C
375°F	191°C
400°F	204°C
425°F	218°C
450°F	232°C

LENGTH

IMPERIAL	METRIC
1 in	2½ cm
2 in	5 cm
4 in	10 cm
6 in	15 cm
8 in	20 cm
10 in	25 cm
12 in	30 cm

KIM LAIDLAW DEDICATION:

To the young people who are courageously exploring who they are with honesty and heart—in a world that doesn't always make it easy—your resilience, creativity, and authenticity light the way for a more compassionate and just future. We see you and honor your journey.

VERONICA HINKE DEDICATION:

Once again, to Mom and Dad.

VERONICA HINKE ACKNOWLEDGMENTS:

I would like to extend sincere thanks to the many people who have been instrumental in some way in the journey to or through this very special book project: Denis Stencil, Debra-Ann Brabazon, Paulette Ennis, Ruth Davis, Jane Olson, Joanna Broder, Janice Harper, Bill Hinke, Shirley Hinke, Florence Weizenicker, Rebecca Lorge, Carrie Quinn, Elaine Hinke, Jeanne Hinke, Jeff Hinke, Ann Michlig, Catherine Mio Anderson, Alex Novak, Nityia Przewlocki, Ruth L. Ratny, Marilee Wright, Eric Alvarado.

ABOUT THE AUTHORS

VERONICA HINKE is a writer, speaker, and journalist, and the author of numerous cookbooks, including *Titanic: The Official Cookbook*, *The Last Night on the Titanic: Unsinkable Drinking, Dining & Style*, and *The Great Gatsby Cooking and Entertaining Guide*. Veronica expertly shares her love of history, literature, and culinary arts through her work.

KIM LAIDLAW is a cookbook author, editor, and recipe developer. She is the author or coauthor of several cookbooks, including bestsellers *The Nightmare Before Christmas: The Official Cookbook & Entertaining Guide*, *Emily in Paris: The Official Cookbook*, and *Five Marys Ranch Raised Cookbook*, as well as the upcoming *Clueless: The Official Cookbook* and numerous Williams Sonoma cookbooks. Her clients also include Disney, Netflix, Weber, Hog Island, KitchenAid, American Girl, and more. She is a former professional baker and baking instructor at the San Francisco Cooking School and owns Cast Iron Media, LLC. Kim lives in Petaluma, California, with her Scottish husband, their always-entertaining daughter, and a bountiful home garden.

INDEX

D

E

F

R

S

T

V

W

PO Box 3088
San Rafael, CA 94912
www.insighteditions.com

Find us on Facebook: www.facebook.com/InsightEditions
Follow us on Instagram: @insighteditions

US Edition ISBN: 979-8-3374-0176-8

Publisher: Raoul Goff
SVP, Group Publisher: Vanessa Lopez
VP, Creative: Chrissy Kwasnik
VP, Manufacturing: Alix Nicholaeff
Editorial Director: Thom O'Hearn
Art Director: Stuart Smith
Senior Designer: Judy Wiatrek Trum
Senior Editor: Eileen Mullan
Editorial Assistant: Melissa Santoyo
VP, Senior Executive Project Editor: Vicki Jaeger
Production Manager: Deena Hashem
Strategic Production Planner: Lina s Palma-Temena

Photographer: Ted Thomas
Food and Prop Stylist: Elena P. Craig
Assistant Food Stylist and Cookie Decorator: Patricia Parrish
Assistant Baker and Candymaker: Lana Mcintire

Illustrations by Warner Bros. and Maryna Kostiushko

REPLANTED PAPER

Insight Editions, in association with Roots of Peace, will plant two trees for each tree used in the manufacturing of this book. Roots of Peace is an internationally renowned humanitarian organization dedicated to eradicating land mines worldwide and converting war-torn lands into productive farms and wildlife habitats. Roots of Peace will plant two million fruit and nut trees in Afghanistan and provide farmers there with the skills and support necessary for sustainable land use.

Manufactured in China by Insight Editions

10 9 8 7 6 5 4 3 2 1